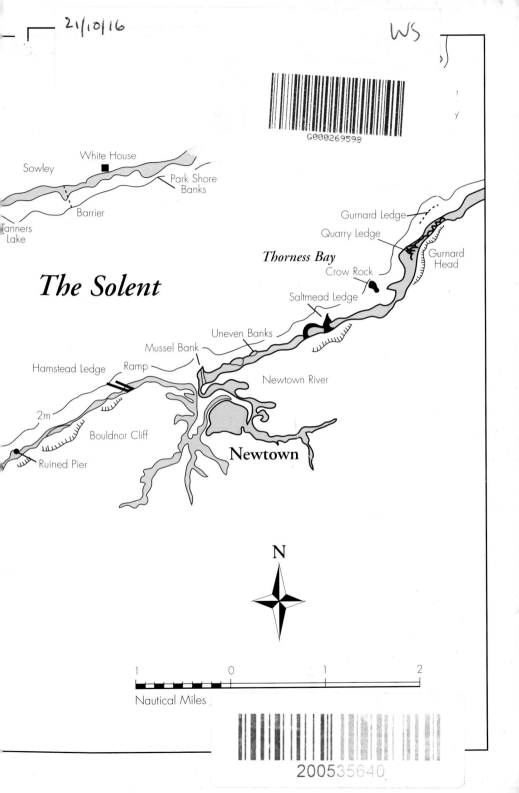

SOLENT
HAZARDS

Peter Bruce

rst edition published May 1985
l edition published November 1985
d edition published October 1987
edition reprinted September 1989
d edition reprinted October 1990
ourth edition published July 1994
rth edition revised November 1997
ifth edition published May 2001
Fifth edition revised June 2003
a edition, second revision April 2008

Other pilotage books by the same author:

Solent Tides
Wight Hazards
Inshore Along the Dorset Coast
Tidal Streams between Portland Bill and St Alban's Head

BOLDRE MARINE
Kestrel Cottage • Shirley Holms • Lymington • Hampshire • SO41 8NH • UK
Telephone & Fax 01590683106

CONTENTS

Acknowledgement
Over the 23 years that *Solent Hazards* has been in print it has grown considerably in content, besides spawning four other similar books. Its life has been a happy and popular one, and I remain tremendously grateful to those who write in with comment or criticism, and particularly those harbourmasters and inshore lifeboatmen who have given up their time for my questions. Also I am equally grateful to the pilots who fly me round the Solent and the learned people who vet the script.

Caution
While every care has been taken in compiling this book, it is regretted that no responsibility can be taken by the author or publisher for inaccuracies or omissions, or for any accidents or mishaps resulting from its use.

Design by David Rose
Printed in China through Printworks Int. Ltd.

Front cover
A yacht aground on Gurnard Ledge. She eventually came off using her spinnaker in reverse.

Back Cover
The *Varvassi* wreck and Goose Rock at a low spring tide.

People ask what has changed since the last edition and, the answer is that as always, changes occur all the time, mostly through human activity.

At the author's request the QHM Portsmouth, Commander Tom Herman, opened a passage in 2005 between No Man's Land Fort and the Island shore that enables small craft to proceed in their own channel clear of large commercial vessels. The passage itself has two metres of water at chart datum and there are now lit posts along the Island shore between Ryde Pier and the Debnigo Shoal.

Another useful contribution to Solent safety by ABP Southampton is to light West Knoll buoy off the Brambles, thus enabling smaller craft on a north-south route, such as Hamble to Cowes and vice versa, to pass close to the Brambles at night in confidence, thereby keeping out of the main shipping channel.

Racing marks in all areas of the Solent are now at last lit, except for some racing marks close in on the Island shore. It would be good eventually to have all Solent floating objects lit, including pot markers.

There has been some change of navigational buoys in the West Solent. In 2006 two new buoys were established, Solent and Lymington Banks, and East Lepe was shifted a little to the south.

The Cowes Harbour Commissioners plan to build a breakwater across the Cowes harbour entrance in 2009, level with the headlands on either side. The breakwater will not be attached to the shore and will have channels giving access from the west and east. The breakwater will give much greater protection from northerly winds and will allow the construction of a large marina on the east side of the river, opposite the Cowes Yacht Haven.

A number of web sites have come into use around the Solent area, giving actual and past weather information. They are at Portland, Hurst, the RLymYC starting platform, Southampton, the Brambles Bank post, Chichester Bar and Chichester Harbour. In addition to the BBC and other forecasts all these can be obtained from the single website *www.scra.org.uk*.

A surprising new hazard seems to have appeared in the narrow channel between the easternmost *Varvassi* boiler and the Needles rocks. In the Round the Island Race of 2007 two racing yachts struck a rusty object there and this difficult passage may have become even more perilous. It is possible that a piece of the *Varvassi's* ship structure may have been driven into the gap by tide or wave action.

Peter Bruce, March 2008

The Solent's sheltered waters have many delights and their popularity is evident. Nevertheless there are features in the Solent that can, from time to time, be a source of inconvenience or worse. This book identifies these hazards, which are mainly under water and, where possible, provides the local knowledge to avoid them, usually with little effort. Such information often involves using transits that, once known, are the surest method of pilotage. Some navigational knowledge is assumed and reference is often made to the relevant Admiralty charts. The book is written for vessels with a draft of up to two metres, though the navigators of deeper vessels may also find the information valuable. Detailed information regarding tidal streams will be found in the tidal stream atlas called 'Solent Tides', also published by Boldre Marine.

When one is struggling against the strong tides of the Solent much advantage can usually be gained by hugging the shore. This often means venturing into shallow water that, without local knowledge, prudent mariners would take care to avoid. How close sailing vessels of a given draft should go to the shore depends upon the height of the tide, the nature of the seabed, and the strength and direction of the wind. For example, if a yacht is beating close to a gently shelving mud bank and the helmsman presses on inshore until he hears or feels the bottom rattle against his keel, then tacks immediately, the yacht's momentum may carry her through the tack. Once heeled on the offshore tack, perhaps aided by moving crew weight, the boat will be on her way again with little disadvantage. Shingle or sand will slow a boat down much more quickly than mud, and even if the helm is put down at the moment of impact she may not pass through the wind before becoming stuck fast. Grounding on rocks or sewer pipes can be a much more harrowing experience, as a yacht will come to an abrupt halt with a chance of injury to crew who were standing up. Even if the yacht has not been obviously holed, the keel bolts may have been strained, or the hull cracked at the forward or after end of the keel. Clearly the margin of safety has to be far greater when sailing near rocks and similar solid objects, especially in a freshening wind and on a falling tide. Whatever she grounds upon, a power vessel will probably sustain expensive damage to propellers and rudders. When near a reef, crews with helmsmen who like to take big risks are advised to sit down and hold on tight.

Some hazards, such as Gurnard Ledge and the Bramble Bank, are well clear of the shore and can be crossed at high water. A good navigator can quickly work out when a yacht can cross in safety: a better one will have worked out beforehand the heights above chart datum at each hour for the expected duration of the race or passage. Computer software which provides this kind of information with great ease is readily available. It is wise to apply a safety margin, as tidal height varies with both wind direction and barometer reading. For example, in the Solent a combination of several days of strong northeasterly wind and a high barometric pressure can lower tidal heights by 0.6m. Note that the higher the barometric pressure the lower the tide and vice versa.

A reliable echo sounder is essential, preferably with a display visible on deck and accurately marked at the point where the vessel will run aground. This can be established when the boat is dried out beside a wall for scrubbing or when she has inadvertently grounded on a flat part of the seabed. It should be remembered that the conventional echo sounder reading will vary a little with angle of heel, and that the transmission will not reflect off the upper layers of soft mud.

Some experienced Solent sailors manage quite well without an echo sounder by looking ahead for abnormal ripples, which may denote shallow water or rocks. For some reason in May, or sometimes June, what the fishermen call 'black water' spreads up to the Solent from the Dorset coast. This water, said to be plankton-rich, is clear, and for a little while one may have an underwater visibility of several metres. During the next four weeks the water becomes gradually more opaque as it reverts to its normal muddy colour. Whilst the 'black water' is present it may be possible to see underwater hazards near the surface.

Should a vessel run aground and not refloat with the use of engine or crew weight, one can often obtain help from passing power craft. Racing yachts have sometimes been rescued from the mud by the wash of passing power vessels. More often power craft, with less draft than a distressed deep-keeled yacht, will offer a tow. If a horizontal pull from the bow or the stern is not successful, the most effective means the assisting craft can use is to tow the grounded yacht broadside on towards deeper water by her spinnaker halyard. In the process the yacht may adopt an alarming angle of heel, but the forces involved are similar to those of a classical spinnaker broach and it is unlikely that any harm will be done. Some generous token of gratitude is usual in the event of success.

Apart from being a wonderful cruising and racing area for leisure craft, the Solent also serves the major commercial port of Southampton. Thus an above-water Solent hazard, no less important than the underwater hazards, is that created by commercial shipping (Plate 1). Restricted by lack of manoeuvrability, lack of forward vision and a draft of up to 14.9m, larger vessels are usually unable to take action to avoid a collision with smaller craft. This applies particularly during a turn, for which a ship may have to maintain a speed of up to 14 knots to achieve satisfactory control around the Bramble Bank or Calshot Spit. Such ships, being constrained by their draft, will show three all-round red lights in a vertical line by night and a cylinder by day. The Southampton Harbour Master's Halmatic 42 or 44-foot (12.8-13.4m) patrol launches may

1

Queen Mary 2's bows from the wrong place to be.
Photo courtesy of Cunard.

escort them, and are readily recognisable by their royal blue hulls, white upper works and broad yellow diagonal stripes showing towards their bows. They use VHF Channel 12, operate blue flashing lights when clearing a path for large commercial vessels, and their officers take a very dim view of yachtsmen mistakenly assuming right of way in the main fairway. A point worth noting is that incoming large vessels proceeding to the Thorn Channel take quite a sharp turn to port towards Gurnard Buoy after passing Prince Consort Buoy, before turning to starboard on the way round West Bramble Buoy. This preliminary turn can be as much as 30° and a sound signal is seldom given.

In 1993 an initiative by the chairman of the Solent Cruising and Racing Association, the quietly effective organisation which looks after the Solent yachtsman's interests, led to the establishment of an 'area of concern' for yachts and small craft, between Black Jack and Reach Buoys off Calshot, to the South Bramble and Prince Consort Buoys off Cowes. In this area of concern small vessels are required to keep out of a moving exclusion area 1000m ahead and 100m on either side of a large vessel using the main channel. Even if apparently clear of the path of an outward-bound vessel, it may still be important to consider which way a vessel is likely to turn. The eastern channel is the more likely, but it is worth knowing that vessels leaving Thorn Channel occasionally display a flag signal to show which channel out of the Solent they intend to take. Flag 'E' (for east) over the answering pendant (or code flag) means that a vessel will be rounding West Bramble buoy and heading eastwards towards the Spithead Forts. Flag 'W' (for west) under the answering pendant means that the vessel will be making westwards for the Needles Channel.

There will normally be a UK pilot on board large vessels using the Port of Southampton. Their working frequencies on VHF are channels 12 and 14. In an emergency one should call on channel 12 and then be ready to shift to another frequency if requested.

In the same area as large deep-draft commercial shipping there is a busy ferry service between Cowes and Southampton. The Red Funnel ferries provide speedy transport, but this means that small vessels have to keep a good lookout both ahead and astern and, at night, ensure that their navigation lights are showing brightly. Dangerous situations can develop rapidly at the sort of speeds the ferries use to maintain their schedules, and it is inadvisable to assume right of way over them.

At one time it was compulsory for

Red Funnel ferries to stay in the main channel between Southampton and Cowes but now, with the permission of the Southampton Harbourmaster, they often take the direct route near the Brambles when the level of the tide allows. Red Funnel operates three modern displacement vehicle-carrying ferries, the 93m *Red Falcon, Red Osprey* and the *Red Eagle*. These were introduced between 1994 and 1996, have Voith Schneider propellers for greater manoeuvrability, and a service speed of 14 knots. Their draft is 2.75m. The three 32m catamarans, *Red Jet 1, 2, & 3* undertake the work on the high-speed route. They were introduced between 1991 and 1998, have a service speed of 36 knots and a draft of 1.4m.

The height of the bridge of the Red Jets is such that at night the masthead navigation lights of yachts are easily lost in the background of shore lights. Maximum illumination is desirable in the area where Red Jets operate, as no radar is infallible.

Regardless of the rule of the road, it is a normal and common courtesy for cruising yachts and power vessels to keep clear of racing yachts. Powerboats should avoid causing wash for racing boats (and indeed everyone else) in light conditions, and both power and cruising vessels should keep to leeward of racing vessels rather than disturb the flow of their wind. It is a normal and common courtesy for racing yachts to thank vessels that have taken the trouble to keep clear of them, even though at times racing crews may feel preoccupied.

Apart from commercial shipping and racing yachts, other floating hazards include unlit racing mark buoys, which are laid in the Solent in summer. The SCRA and RLymYC buoys are all lit, have a characteristic Fl Amber 4s, as are most of the racing mark buoys in APB Southampton and QHM Portsmouth areas within the Solent. Use of reflective tape has improved the unlit buoys' visibility, but when the night is too dark to see ahead, or in thick fog without radar, one needs to plot a course to be sure of clearing them.

To describe the hazards of the Solent, an imaginary voyage will be taken, with the aid of Admiralty Charts 2035, 2036 and 2037, from Cowes westward up the Island coast to the Needles, across to the Shingles Bank and then eastwards along the Hampshire shore to the Spithead Forts and finally back up the Island shore again to Cowes. Most of the photographs used to illustrate the main features were taken at exceptionally low spring tides and show the coastal features near chart datum.

The Cowes area of the Solent has long been famous for first-class racing in waters where local knowledge can count heavily. Every year the general standard of competition seems to improve, bringing greater pressure on helmsmen to know precisely where they can sail and where they cannot.

COWES GREEN

Cowes Green, that part of the West Cowes shoreline between the Royal Yacht Squadron and Egypt Point, is one of the most popular vantage points to watch the competitors in sailing regattas such as Cowes Week. Here spectators are sometimes given a remarkable display of close-quarters racing with the competing yachts only a biscuit toss from the beach. This happens when the vagaries of the Solent sea breeze cause a large part of the racing fleet to bunch at a down-tide turning mark in the West Solent. Each boat then has to work up the shore under spinnaker towards the finishing line against the tide. On these occasions the anguish of the competitors can be appreciated from some of the rich language that may waft its way to the shore. As if this were not enough

2

The RYS harbour is a benefit to Cowes. It enables the Trinity Landing out of the picture to the south to withstand northerly storms, apart from providing a good base for committee boats during regattas. The annotation LION ROCKS marks a reef opposite the RYS Pavilion that has been known to impede keelboats. The fairway side of the Trinity Landing pontoon is available for short stays by vessels that remain manned.

Photo © Alastair Badman

LION ROCKS

entertainment, there is also a good chance that one or two competitors, hoping to minimise the effect of the contrary tide, or to clear their wind from the boats behind, will come too close to one of several rocks that exist off Cowes Green. On a falling tide this may be where they end their day, as happened to a Prince of the Realm in Cowes Week 1992. Embarrassment such as this can readily be avoided by observance of the simple transit described in the next paragraph.

The first hazard to note, when heading west from Number One Buoy at Cowes harbour entrance, is a reef close in under the shore opposite the eastern end of the Royal Yacht Squadron garden, sometimes known as Lion Rock (Plate 2). Grantham Rocks, a little further to the west, are in the shape of a hollow cone lying along the shore with its apex towards Egypt Point. The rocks extend furthest out opposite the houses built closest to the shore (Plate 3). It is quite easy to become stuck on the outside of Grantham Rocks, or even be trapped in the hollow of the cone when cheating the tide along this shore. Fortunately there is a simple rule for the avoidance of both Lion Rock and the entire Grantham Rocks ledge: the white painted structure at Egypt Point, which is all that remains of the old light, is easy to identify, and some

3

Cowes Green and Grantham rocks.

25m to the east there is a statue of a semi-rampant lion on a plinth. A transit between the Egypt Point light structure, while it still remains, and the lion on 272°M takes a yacht down a line just outside the outer limit of all these rocks (Plate 4).

The beach is clear of major rocks to the west of the beach shelter with its pyramid-shaped roof, though it is wise to go outside the post marking the council slipway opposite the New Holmwood Hotel. One can then safely go close in at Egypt Point itself, but one cannot do so to the west of the point.

4 (above)
Looking west at the transit between the old Egypt Light structure and the statue of a semi-rampart lion. The post with the green cone marks the end of a slipway.

GURNARD BAY

As far as navigation is concerned the salient feature of Gurnard Bay is Gurnard Ledge (Plate 5). This ledge is composed of clay and limestone, and appears at extreme low springs in the

5 (below)
Gurnard Ledge and Gurnard Ledge Buoy.

middle of Gurnard Bay running west-wards towards Thorness Bay. When coming from the direction of Egypt Point it is easy to find the gap between the ledge and the shore on the way in, but it is not always so easy to find the gap at the west end on the way out. The ledge is not an obvious hazard: it is well out in the tideway, steep-to, and whilst the Gurnard Ledge buoy is clear enough, it can be difficult to judge where the ledge itself is. Occasionally fish floats are laid at some point along the ledge, which can be helpful, as is the yellowy colour in the water appearing down-tide from the ledge, caused by the erosion of the clay. The eastern end of Gurnard Ledge is in line with the Gurnard Sailing Club flagstaff and the third window from the right of the large building on 086°M, a hotel called The Woodvale (Plate 6). This transit is particularly useful when a decision has been made to pass outside Gurnard Ledge but inside the Gurnard Ledge

6

The east end of Gurnard Ledge is in line with the Gurnard Sailing Club flagpole and the third window from right of the Woodvale Hotel.

buoy. Another transit to indicate the eastern end of the ledge is not easy to find. However there is a yellow diamond beacon at the Gurnard Luck estuary just to the left of a prominent house with a picture window above a high sea wall. This, aligned with the distant roofs of the white Gurnard Pines holiday camp buildings, gives a rough east-west position (Plate 7). There is no convenient transit

7

The east end of Gurnard Ledge is also in line with the yellow diamond beacon by the Gurnard Luck estuary and the distant holiday camp buildings, to be seen in this photograph to the right of the post.

8

A northeast-southwest course near to Baxter's buoy may find slightly deeper water between Gurnard Ledge and the Island shore, but there is generally less than 1 m at datum and, for many vessels, the passage will be impassable at times.

for finding the deepest water at the west end of the inshore passage, but some guidance is given by a round white dinghy racing buoy with a white pole top mark called Baxters, which is laid in summer off Quarry Ledge (or Baxter's Ledge, as it is known locally) (Plate 8). On a northeast-southwest course in the area of Baxter's buoy, Gurnard Ledge is lower than offshore. The deepest water, perhaps half a metre more, is to be found when the top of the Gurnard Sailing Club mast is just to the left of the prominent white gable end central attic window of the house due east of the mast.

Because of the infamous ledge, Cowes race officers usually avoid setting courses which take yachts into Gurnard Bay immediately after the start; but circumstances may be such that com-peting yachts become drawn in there later on in the race to avoid the tide. For example, many of the yachts taking part in the first race of the 1981 and 1993 Admiral's Cups went aground on Gurnard Ledge. In 1977 *Big Apple* and in 1987 *Blizzard*, with well-known skippers at the helm, came to dramatic halts on its eastern corner. More recently the Irish Team Admiral's Cup yacht *Jameson 1*, owned by King Harald of Norway and, incidentally, skippered by the same helmsman who was in *Big Apple* in 1977, sank there after going aground on 29 July 1993. Other yachts in the race were severely damaged. If there is not enough water over Gurnard Ledge to ignore it altogether, a decision has to be made whether to take the inshore passage inside Gurnard Ledge, or to pass outside it. Close to high water most yachts can tack with some confidence inside the ledge along the shore round to Quarry (aka Baxter's) Ledge. Even so, the inshore route

9 (left)

To the west of Egypt Point there are reefs off Briary Court, just to the right of centre, and Hawkins House, further to the right.

10 (below)

At the east end of Gurnard Bay more prominent reefs start at the gas pressure reduction station, the building on the left that cuts into the greenery above the road.

should not be undertaken lightly.

When working along the shore west from Egypt Point, one should take into account two series of rock outcrops. The first of these lurks just round the corner from Egypt Point opposite Briary Court and Hawkins House (Plate 9). This includes some

wreckage, reputedly of a German bomber – one of the less lucky ones that gave Cowes a pasting during World War II. The second reef lies off the gas pressure-reduction station – a flat-roofed building above road level – and continues to the southwest as far as the white Gurnard Sailing Club

There is seldom a good reason to steer close to the shore at the centre of Gurnard Bay. The yacht in the centre of the picture is on a good line.

(Plate 10). Of these the first rocks to uncover lie between the 'gas station' and the green-roofed bungalow.

A number of newer groynes, which are well marked with posts and topmarks, have been built along the southeast shore of Gurnard Bay and the reef runs roughly parallel to the shore, some 50m further out from the line of posts. New storm water pipes, marked with a green triangle-topped post, were laid in 2000 on the east side of Gurnard Bay, opposite the point where Princes Esplanade reaches the level of the beach. The discharge is 400m out from the shore and the pipes are entirely buried. The construction of this outfall replaced the two above-seabed Gurnard sewer pipes, that later were used as storm overflow pipes. Southern Water intended to remove the redundant Woodvale pipe off Gurnard Sailing Club and the pipe off Gurnard Marsh (Plate 11) but this was not allowed by Natural England on conservation grounds. Beyond the Gurnard Sailing Club a reef comes out from the shore on the south side of the bay (Plate 11). Two white 0.9m diameter buoys laid off the Gurnard Sailing Club, which are the outer distance marks of the dinghy starting line, roughly mark this. Before this reef becomes a problem, however, it will be found that one is out of the main tidal stream and it is time to look for the deeper water to the west.

Alter course to south west off the

2

Gurnard Sailing Club, assuming one is taking the inshore channel, and make sure that the Woodvale Hotel remains just in sight when one comes to the promontory off Gurnard Ledge buoy. The navigationally useful Salty Seadog restaurant buoys are no longer laid.

If one does want to go inshore, there is a mostly covered cable (Plate 11) running across the reef to the west of the Gurnard Sailing Club, which reaches the shore not far from the inner end of another old Gurnard Bay pipe at Gurnard Marsh. This is also unmarked, but runs under the seabed after some 80m. Just to the west there are pedestals and a larger concrete block still remaining from two

12

A post marks the concrete block and other salient remains of the old Gurnard Marsh outfalls.

Gurnard Marsh pipes that have mostly been removed. The pedestals show well above the seabed and constitute a slight hazard. Of more significance is

13

The Gurnard Luck estuary and, beyond, Cooks Bay.

a large concrete block – that may have provided a manhole in the past – which is marked with a post and green triangle (Plate 12). Clearly, all but racing dinghies will want to avoid such complications by keeping to seaward, though not so far out as Gurnard Ledge.

The Gurnard Luck river estuary (Plate 13) lies between the prominent glass-fronted house and a yellow diamond-headed post to the west, and the Dart 15 club with its forest of masts to the east. The river is packed with small shallow-draft fishing boats, in the short reach up to the road bridge. These can pass to and from the Solent for a period of about five hours around high water (Plate 14). Prisoners escaping from one of the island's gaols were sometimes believed to be making for

14

Gurnard Luck moorings. Notice the diamond-topped post, which can be used as a transit to mark the east end of Gurnard Ledge.

The Luck to commandeer a boat to escape to the mainland, and the rather overgrown seat where the warders used to wait for them can still be seen.

To the west of the Gurnard Marsh storm water outfall the shore of Cooks Bay looks rockbound at high water. In fact, the rocks along the shore give way to sand not far beneath the surface and there are no surprises close to the shore until Gurnard Head itself has been reached, unless one tries to anchor. In this event the newly-laid power cable marked, as is normal, by a yellow diamond-topped post, seems to catch ground tackle rather frequently.

THORNESS BAY

At Gurnard Head, the promontory between Gurnard and Thorness Bays, Quarry Ledge, or Baxter's Ledge as the locals prefer to call it, sticks out like a clenched fist 220m from the shore (Plates 15 and 16). It can catch those keen to reach the weaker tides of Thorness Bay, who come in from the east following soundings, and then can be trapped within the indentation on the north side.

A clearing bearing of Quarry (Baxter's) Ledge is 066°M on the Woodvale Hotel, which is when it is in full view. Another useful transit that clips the western outer edge of the ledge is found by lining up the

15 (above)

Quarrie (Baxter's) Ledge, looking south.

16 (below)

Quarrie (Baxter's) Ledge, looking east.

17

To be clear of Quarrie (Baxter's) Ledge, keep outside the transit of Rowridge TV tower and Little Thorness Farmhouse.

Rowridge TV mast with Little Thorness farmhouse on about 192°M (Plate 17). This is a double-layer red-roofed house to the right of a bungalow. The lower level red roof looks like a covered-over veranda, which is what it is.

Apart from Quarry Ledge there are other ledges to beware of in Thorness Bay. A line of rocks stretches out from the shore towards the centre of the bay and some way to seaward of this there is an isolated patch of rocks (Plate 18). Both of these hazards may be recognised by fish floats, surface weed or choppy water over them. The outer patch of rocks, called Crow Rock – or Diamond Rocks – is usually the one to worry about (Plate 19). It can be found by lining up Rowridge TV tower with the left-hand corner of the Thorness Bay Holiday Park 'Cruisers Club' on a bearing of 190°M. The building is painted pale yellow, with a glass conservatory on its

18

Looking WNW into Thorness Bay. Quarrie (Baxter's) Ledge is on the right and the central ledge on the left.

19

Crow Rock in the foreground and the central ledge of Thorness Bay in the background on the left.

right hand side. To be to seaward of these rocks, keep a bunch of two-storey light coloured buildings in sight to the left of Gurnard Head on about 057°M. If no buildings are in sight, and there is a breeze, sit down and hold on tight.

Towards the wooded part of the shore there is a bank of rocks with a post in the midst of them. This marks a disused sewer outfall coming from the adjoining holiday centre (Plate 20). This post does, by chance, help to mark the rock ledge as well. Further west yet another rock ledge extends seawards from the shore before one reaches Salt Mead. The ledge lies opposite the part of the coast where a lumpy incline of bare soil and scrub leads up to trees on the skyline.

There are no high-profile rocks amongst the ledges described thus far, nor is there great tidal advantage to be gained once inside the line of Gurnard Head and Hamstead Point. Consequently it is as well not to try to work this shore too closely, even at high tide, when strings of seaweed from the ledges float to the surface. Nevertheless in both Thorness and Gurnard Bays small craft may want to take advantage of an east-going eddy. This is to be found close to the shore at spring tides from two to five hours

20

The rock ledge at the west end of Thorness Bay, looking north west.

after high water Portsmouth.

A lagoon forms at high tide on the Thorness Bay shore, which is deep enough to be used for fishing boat moorings (Plate 21). The lagoon makes a good high water dinghy-landing place in choppy sea conditions. Another shore feature to the east of the lagoon and visible at low tide is the Solo pipe manifold and supply pipes running over the seabed from Lepe. These pipes were laid in World War II for the top secret Pluto project, the successful undersea pipeline that supplied fuel to the Allied armies after D Day.

21 (right)

The Thorness Bay lagoon at low water.

SALT MEAD LEDGE

Salt Mead Ledge (Plate 22) can come as a surprise when approached from either direction, so an early offing may be necessary. Rather than running at right angles to the shore, as indicated on old charts, the ledge inclines towards Cowes. Thus when beating westwards on soundings from Thorness Bay, it is possible to encounter Salt Mead Ledge with the keel on the offshore tack. The ledge is steep on its western side so, when coming from the west, avoiding action may be necessary before soundings give warning. The ledge extends further out underwater than the photograph indicates, its extremity being often marked by fishing floats and choppy sea. It is worth remembering that the ledge lies opposite Burnt Wood, another plantation that comes down to the shore (Plate 22 and 23). A clearing transit for Salt Mead Ledge is not at all easy to find. When they can be seen, the distant Hamstead Point and the red port hand Newtown River outer entrance buoy on approximately 252°M clears most, but not all, of the ledge (Plate 24).

Just to the west of Salt Mead lies a semi-circular pattern of rocks (Plate 25), and beyond this some changeable sandbanks before a mussel bank

22

Salt Mead Ledge looking north. Salt Mead Ledge buoy can just be seen in the top left corner.

23

A closer view of Salt Mead Ledge with Burnt Wood behind.

24

The clearing transit on Salt Mead Ledge. The red Newtown fairway buoy should be kept inside Hamstead Point.

running northwards from the shore about 200m short of the Newtown River entrance (Plate 27).

NEWTOWN

Newtown is one of the most beautiful and popular anchorages in the Solent. The town was esteemed by the Romans for the quality of its oysters and was once the capital of the Island. It was comprehensively burnt down by the French in 1377 and though rebuilt it never recovered its previous prosperity. Many yachtsmen go there to pick

25 (opposite page)

Looking northeast from the semi-circular rock pattern off Salt Mead, back to Quarry Ledge.

26 (above)

Banks to the east of Newtown.

27 (below)

Looking northeast from Newtown River entrance. The yacht on the left did not quite find the channel.

up a mooring, or to anchor inside or outside, for lunch. From the red fairway buoy (characteristic Fl.R.4s) there is not much over a metre in the channel at chart datum, which allows most keelboats in, except at an extreme low spring tide. The leading marks should be disregarded soon after passing the red buoy, and a course taken for the entrance keeping well to starboard in the narrow channel when there are other craft about. The harbour master's phone number is 01983531622.

There are rewarding high water dinghy expeditions to Clamerkin Lake, to Western Haven (Plate 28), to Shalfeet and to Causeway Lake. There are four landing places. Firstly at the beach to be seen on the right of the entrance, called the Hamstead Duver, which is useable at any state of the tide. Also one can land at Newtown Quay to view the site of the town itself. This is up the western arm of the river towards Causeway Lake, near the black shed behind which a fresh water tap is to be found. One can land also at Hamstead Jetty on the right hand side of the western river roughly opposite Newtown Quay, and from where one can pick up the coastal path. Finally one can land at Shalfleet Quay, from where one can walk to the New Inn and the village. In the last three cases, landing is best at three hours either side of high water. Note also, if

under oars, that on the last three hours of a spring ebb the tide comes out of Newtown River entrance at a gallop. Newtown is a nature reserve: watch out for red squirrels, the silver-washed fritillary, the green-winged orchid and the Mediterranean gull. In spring and autumn ospreys often pass through.

There is a busy small arms firing range on the east side of Newtown, not only used by the reserve forces who own and administer it, but also by the regular army, the special services, the Royal Marines, the police, the coast-guards and rifle clubs. Do not go up the lake beyond the mooring buoys or pass within 200m of the shore on the seaward side when red flags are flying, as live firing is taking place. One flag-pole will be seen at Shepherd's Hill, opposite Saltmead buoy, and the other two above the small cliffs on the eastern arm of Newtown entrance. Live firing only takes place on Wednesdays, Thursdays, Saturdays and Sundays.

In the summer, particularly at weekends, Newtown becomes very crowded, sometimes impossibly so. This contrasts with winter when one often has Newtown to oneself, apart from the large population of wildfowl, particularly Brent geese.

3

HAMSTEAD LEDGE

At Hamstead Point, the shore can be approached using an echo sounder until opposite a large concrete ramp at a gap in the trees, which has been built at high water level. This ramp is at the site of the boom defence depot in the last world war where flotation buoys were probably launched for the boom between the Hamstead Point barrier in the south, and the Durns Point barrier in the north. The ramp was also used for tank landing practice. Though still marked on the chart, the Hamstead Point barrier was mostly removed in 1996. Two stumps remain inshore.

Hamstead Ledge buoy marks a deep ledge of minimum depth 7.6m. Well inshore of the buoy are two parallel bars of Bembridge limestone (Plate 29) that are of more interest to owners of leisure craft. These extend westward at an acute angle to the shore. The inner bar is longest and extends further out than the outer bar, and there is only about 0.4m depth over the tip at chart datum. Minor parallel bars lie inshore and extend further to the west.

Until it was removed, the barrier served moderately well to mark the ledges. Now it is not so easy to judge where they are, and an echo sounder will give very little warning. One may assume that the root of the ledge starts from the concrete slipway, and the outer extremity of the ledges ends approximately opposite the east end of the pinewood on the top of the cliff.

29

The ledges off Hamstead Point, looking south.

30

To avoid the ledges off Hamstead Point, stay north of the transit of the BAE Systems Nearfield Tower and the left hand tip of Burnt Wood on a bearing of 080°.

A good clearing transit would be especially helpful as the depth drops from 10m to nothing very abruptly due to a submerged clay cliff that runs parallel to the shore between Newtown and Yarmouth. The platform at the bottom of this cliff is covered with tree stumps from ancient forest that grew along the shore as it was 8500 years ago. Worked flints have also been found. Again there is no easy transit to avoid the ledges, but the most satisfactory is to keep north of a line between the distant BAE Systems concrete cylindrical Nearfield test facility tower, which can just be seen above the skyline in clear weather, and the promontory at Salt Mead where the Burnt Wood trees go down to sea level on 080°M (Plate 30).

BOULDNOR CLIFF SHORE

Between Hamstead Ledge and Yarmouth Pier the shore is uneven with occasional rocky patches (Plate 31) and three sand spits. There are two off-lying

31

Bouldnor shore.

32

The remnants of the stone pier off Bouldnor.

33

The shoreline off Bouldnor, looking east towards Hamstead Point. The remaining piece of stone pier wall shows up as a light-coloured speck against the dark seaweed covered base. Note the three sand bars, one to the east of the stone pier, and two to the west.

features, a ruined stone pier and an obstruction called The Camel.

Five hundred metres off the west end of Bouldnor Cliff, shown at a depth of 6.3m, lies the wreck of a gravel dredger, the *Margaret Smith*, which capsized on 28 June 1978 after her cargo had shifted. Inshore of her can be seen the remnants of the stone pier which was constructed in the 19th century for loading bricks made in kilns nearby. All that now remains is a square-shaped base 65m from the cliff face, on which a stone wall stands, rising about 5m above the surrounding sea bed level (Plate 32). The wall, which is never covered at high water, runs north-south and, whilst coming as something of a surprise, what is left of this old and rather beautifully-laid masonry does not extend significantly beyond what can be seen. Thus a very shallow-drafted craft can even pass between the ruins and the shore at high water, but be careful of the sand spit to the east. Not far beyond the stone pier to the east a stream, marked by reeds, can be seen on the shore. Offshore of the stream a sand and mud bar forms an island at low water.

Further on, one mile east from Yarmouth Pier, another sand spit sticks out from a point to the east of the private slipway at Eastmore House (Plate 33). The particular tree that used to mark the spit has fallen down the cliff but will still be visible on the beach for a little while. Otherwise one can

34

The shore off Eastmore House dries out some way.

35

The Camel can be seen in the centre of the
photograph as a high point to the right of the ledge.

assume that the spit lies about half way
along the yellowy cliff face (Plate 34).

Less than half a mile east of
Yarmouth Pier, opposite a point shown
on the chart where the Wilmingham
Road intersects with the coast road, a
bank of 0.8m depth extends 425m offshore (Plate 35). The bank needs to be
given a generous allowance at low
water; moreover an isolated hump on
it, thought to be made of concrete and
known as The Camel (Plate 36); dries
0.4m at chart datum. This obstruction
is roughly 1.5m across and protrudes
about half a metre above the surrounding depth. At present it is marked by a
40cm diameter green buoy. The Camel
is situated on a flattish rock ledge
about 170m from the shore, and can

36 (above)

The Camel showing at low water spring tide. Note
the abutment in the sea wall and the beige (once
pink) house behind it.

be found by lining up the end of Yarmouth Pier with the distant boarded-up coastguard look-out tower at Hurst on a bearing of 272°M. Then one may proceed until the eastern gable of the beige house, called Waterside, which stands at the western end of the buildings on the shore, is in line with the nearby abutment in the sea wall, on a bearing of 181°M. Should the abutment not be easily visible, the large oak tree in front of the house serves equally well as an alternative, so long as it remains there. One can be sure of being clear to the north of the Camel and the outlying rocks on the same plateau by keeping all of Hurst Spit fully in view to the right of Yarmouth Pier.

Four hundred metres east of Yarmouth Pier, and at a depth of about 5m, lies a 16th century protected wreck, marked by a large yellow buoy. She has been fairly certainly identified as the Spanish merchant vessel *Santa Lucia*, which records show sank off Yarmouth in 1567 when bound for Flanders with a cargo of wool. At this time there was busy trade of the fine Spanish merino wool to the looms of Flanders, but it is unlikely that the *Santa Lucia* would have entered the Solent without a pressing reason. By 1567 relations between Spain and England had soured, not least due to English buccaneering

activities. The Spanish well knew that the very active pirates, mainly Flemish and Dutch, but also including many English, known as the *Gueux*, used the Solent as a base (see page 100). At that time the Island was thick with them, gentlemen included, so it seems possible that, at some point, the *Santa Lucia* was captured by pirates. It is significant that Sir Edward Horsey, Captain of the Isle of Wight, whose attitude to piracy can best be described as ambivalent, recovered the cargo. There is no record of what happened to the crew.

YARMOUTH

The charming little town of Yarmouth has always been a very popular port for mariners. It has good shore facilities and is a most convenient point of departure for those bound down channel.

It is a regrettable fact that, on rare occasions, fishermen on Yarmouth Pier have been known to hook passing yachtsmen, so it is wise to be on guard when sailing close to the end of the pier. As a result of these occurrences there is a notice to the effect that seafarers have a right to pass close to the Yarmouth Pier Head, and have right of way over fishing lines.

Note that when a square red flag is flown or an illuminated sign saying 'harbour full' is displayed at the har-

37

Yarmouth.

bour entrance it means that Yarmouth inner harbour is full; though some of the 38 moorings to be had outside the harbour may still be available (Plate 37). The intention of the signal is to save vessels from having to turn round in the narrow entrance of the harbour.

In May 2000 east and west lit fairway buoys were established outside the line of the pier head. The western buoy was permanently removed in 2002 when it was found to be too much of an obstacle for the ferry. A line from the eastern buoy towards Black Rock now delineates the 6K speed limit that applies in the harbour mouth and within the visitors' moorings to the west. East-west traffic should keep to the north of this line.

There are 250 visitors' moorings inside the harbour where the speed limit is 4 knots. A water taxi service operates between 8am and midnight for 52 weeks of the year. They can be contacted on VHF channel 15 or by calling 01983760766. The swing bridge will open in the summer on request at nine set times during the day. Call on VHF channel 68, callsign Yar Bridge.

The lovely Yar River is worth exploring by dinghy at high water (Plate 38).

38

The upper reaches of the Yar River.

39 (above)

Black Rock can be seen on the right and Black Rock Buoy is on the left hand edge of the photograph.

YARMOUTH ROAD

The principal hazard in Yarmouth Road is the rocky plateau known as Black Rock (Plate 39) that lies about half way between the Black Rock Buoy and the shore. It is roughly triangular in plan, with a 70m base running parallel with the shore, and a 20m apex pointing south. A clearing bearing is 97°M on the end of Yarmouth Pier. As an alternative to using a hand-bearing compass, one can devise another transit by using the end of Yarmouth Pier again and ensuring that the end of the pier lines up on the deciduous trees behind, rather than the gently sloping conifers on the sky-line (Plate 40). Black Rock buoy has been lit since October 1997 (Fl. G. 5sec).

40

Black Rock can be cleared by keeping the end of Yarmouth Pier in line with the nearer deciduous trees of Bouldnor, rather than the more distant pine trees on the skyline. This line takes a vessel well inside Black Rock buoy but clear of Black Rock.

Inside Black Rock there is a wide and shallow inner passage, and this may be used at high water on the way to and from Yarmouth Harbour, but care should be taken to avoid lumps

41

A transit between the end of Victoria Pier and the lookout tower at Hurst gives the deepest water in the channel between Black Rock and the Yarmouth shore. Most craft can only use this channel at high water.

The longer one, just to the west of Black Rock, was constructed in 1980 and is mostly buried. The shorter pipe, marked 'Disused' on old charts, is sometimes partly exposed above the seabed level near to the shore. A yellow spherical buoy has been marking the end of the pipe since 1997.

SCONCE POINT TO WARDEN POINT

opposite the breakwater, which dry out at low water springs. To the west of the breakwater the dilapidated Victoria Pier provides a transit for the high water inshore passage. Line up the end of the pier with the lookout tower at Hurst Point on 272°M (Plate 41).

Two unmarked pipes, shown on the chart, run out to sea from Norton.

One can approach the beach closely at Sconce Point, but further west, where a useful little eddy forms on the ebb, the shore shelves less steeply. There is a sprinkling of small rocks on the beach about half way between Sconce and Round Tower Point, and between

42

Looking southwest at Round Tower Point on the left and Fort Albert on the right.

43

The prominent rocks off Round Tower Point are cleared by keeping the distant old coastguard cottages on West High Down in view to the right of Fort Albert, as shown in this photograph.

Round Tower Point and Fort Albert there are spits of rock and sand. Of more significance are the prominent rocks, not shown on the chart, that lie off Round Tower Point itself (Plate 42). The outermost rock is on a line between the right-hand side of Fort Albert, and the cleft in the skyline created by the dry moat at the Needles Old Battery. The rocks off Round Tower Point are safely inshore if a vessel is north of a transit between the square outline of the old coastguard cottages on the skyline at Tennyson Down - or, to be more exact, West High Down - and the right-hand wall of Fort Albert (Plate 43).

There is a wreck of a small tug which was bombed in World War II lying buried in the sand between Round Tower Point and Fort Albert. Her diesel engine has toppled over, but still projects nearly a metre above the surrounding sand level.

Another spit of low-profile rocks, extending north from the north jetty of Fort Albert, can catch out craft coming in from the Needles. Local fishermen call this Fort Albert Ledge (Plate 44). If Tennyson's Cross is

44

Fort Albert and its ledge. How Reef can be seen in the background.

45 (above)

How Reef looking NNW.

46 (below)

Colwell Bay.

visible a fort's width outside the right-hand edge of the fort one is on the edge of deep water.

Charts show How Bank, How Ledge and How Reef in Colwell Bay to the west of Fort Albert (Plate 45). Viewed from the air, the submerged ledge can clearly be seen, usually marked by a number of lobster pot floats. To the northeast of the tip of How Ledge a more isolated rock exists not far beneath the surface. There has been a report of another isolated submerged rock about 200m to the northeast, but there is no corroboration of the drying patch shown on the chart towards Fort Albert. Thus when seeking to anchor in the shallow and tricky Colwell Bay, an approach is best made from the north (Plate 46).

Warden Ledge, which divides Colwell Bay from Totland Bay, is

much like How Ledge but on a larger scale and more prominent (Plate 47).

47

Warden Ledge.

If passing inside Warden Ledge buoy there are four 10k speed limit buoys to consider as well as Warden Ledge itself, where floats and choppy water caused by the tidal stream should roughly indicate its whereabouts. However there is also a most useful transit on a bearing of 222°M between the cleft on the skyline and Hatherwood Point, giving at least two metres over How Bank, How Ledge and Warden Ledge, except perhaps on an unusually low tide (Plate 48). When edging in towards Colwell Bay and Totland Bay to avoid the full strength of a contrary tide on the way out of the Solent this transit becomes especially valuable. When returning to the Solent one should keep Sconce Buoy in view to the left of Fort Albert.

On 4 May 1989 the maxi-yacht *Belmont* (ex-UBS), a one-time Whitbread Round the World Race winner of about 3.5m draft, was carrying out sailing trials in the Needles Channel in company with another maxi-yacht called *Rothmans*. *Belmont* struck a rock off Warden Ledge an hour before low water spring tide and as a result of this stranding her navigator was sacked. Michael Wason of Totland took careful transits, supported by photographs, and from these it seems likely that Belmont had encountered an uncharted rock outside the five metre line. The skipper of Belmont was made aware of this possible defence, but the navigator was not reinstated.

48

By keeping north of a line between Hatherwood Point and the cleft in the skyline on a bearing of 222°M, vessels of moderate draft will be clear of all the rocks in Colwell and Totland Bays.

49
The anchorage in Totland Bay.

TOTLAND BAY

Once well past Warden Ledge, the pleasant anchorage at Totland Bay is clear of offshore rocks (Plate 49), but to the west of the bay there is a reef lying parallel to the shore some 100m out, which begins 750m southwest of the pier. The bigger rocks at the east end of this reef are called the Upper Penner and the Lower Penner. The iron post, shown on older charts 100m to the southeast of the Penner Rocks, has long since gone. A transit to clear the Penner Rocks very comfortably is given by a pair of specially painted white posts at the lower end of the flight of steps at Widdick Chine. The steps are just to the west of the old lifeboat house, the isolated blue-doored building above the sea wall. A buoyed oak tree trunk has embedded itself inshore just east of the lifeboat house, and is hazardous.

To the west of the Penners there is a dense semi-circular pattern of rocks, and then a separate cluster. The reef is about 350m long, and beyond it the coast remains rocky, particularly off Hatherwood Point. The rocky shore continues round into Alum Bay to just short of the chair lift (Plate 50).

50
Looking east at the rocky coastline between
Hatherwood Point and Totland Bay.

ALUM BAY

Alum Bay. East Long Rock can be seen on the right.

Alum Bay is a popular daytime anchorage. It is sheltered from anything south of west through to east and is subject only to gentle tidal streams. On the approach from the east the 'Hatherwood Rock', shown on the chart, which also used to be known by some local fishermen as Five Fingers Rock, has fragmented leaving plenty of nasty inshore rocks on this corner. For example Five Fingers Rock, as charted, has a depth of only 1m.

There is now nothing left to see above water of the original Alum Bay Pier, which was built in the latter half of the nineteenth century. It started to collapse in 1927, then was partially demolished in 1942 so that enemy invaders could not use it. The outer pier post, which was leaning at a drunken angle for many years, disap-

peared in 1992. Though perhaps not quite horizontal, it is said to be well covered. Two upright submerged stumps, just 2m and 7m inshore of where the outer post used to be, may still exist, as well as other pier remnants on the seabed that tend to catch ground tackle. A small new pier was built to the south of the old one in April 1987.

Of greater concern than the remnants of the old pier are the offshore rocks, 200m apart, rising sharply some 5m from a flat seabed (Plate 51). The western one, described as The Long Rock (dr 1.2m) on older charts, is in the form of two lengths that never quite show. Modern charts show it with a charted depth of 0.4m, which seems about right (Plate 52). The eastern rock, which runs like a peaked wall for about 20m, parallel to the Needles,

52

Looking into the corner of Alum Bay. East Long Rock can be seen left of centre, and the submerged West Long Rock can just be seen to the right of centre.

53

East Long Rock awash at low water springs. Note that the white column of the chair lift base lines up with the end of the pier.

appears at an average low water spring tide, and modern charts show it as drying 0.9m (Plate 53). They also now show it north of the 50°40'N line rather than south, as before. Michael Wason has taken measurements that suggest that the original position was correct. This is borne out by aerial photos that show both Long Rocks running parallel to the southern cliff, less than half the distance from the cliff to the bottom of the chair lift. The rocks are slightly staggered, with East Long Rock to the south. The highest point of both rocks is at their western ends. There is yet another rock in line with both of them to the west, marked on the chart, that has 2.2m depth on old charts, and 1.5m on newer ones.

Ian Watling, the owner of the 1987 jetty and of the Needles pleasure boat *'Wild Rose'* has placed a yellow marker can just to the northwest of the East Long Rock. Nevertheless visiting vessels continue to hit the rock and Ian Watling relates the story of the bowman, ready with his anchor, who fell over his bow into the sea when his vessel came to a sudden halt on the rock. A fishing float sometimes marks the western Long Rock, otherwise it is difficult to place. It is helpful to know that if the left-hand end of the Hurst fortifications is in line with the toe of Hatherwood Point, one is between East and West Long Rock; a line from the right hand end of Hurst fortifications to the toe of Hatherwood Point takes one close to the east side of West Long Rock. Approximate bearings from western Long Rock are: top of chair-lift pylon 068°M, chimney of house in corner of cliff 103°M, right-hand chimney pot of the old coast guard cottages on West High Down 201°M, and Needles light 253°M. On this latter bearing the bottom right-hand corner of the central red band of the lighthouse is roughly in line with the right-hand sloping edge of the outer Needle at low water.

Inside the Long Rocks, in the very corner of Alum Bay, there is a ledge called Plattagen Rocks, which never quite dries. A Fairmile launch was beached there in the early seventies after hitting the Mid Shingles buoy in the night, and some parts of her, notably a propeller shaft, still remain.

Six hundred metres west of the corner of Alum Bay, about 35m from the foot of the cliff, there is an iron post lying horizontally eastwards that dries about 1m at chart datum, and is thus able to give another nasty surprise to those venturing very close to the shore. The post is believed to be the remains of a pre-war practice target and is toppling over a little more every year.

Since the Needles lighthouse was automated in 1994, the 800m power supply cable has had a rather chequered life. The cable emerges from the cliff beneath the Needles Battery and leads to the lighthouse along the seabed, parallel to the shore. The causes of the breakages remain a mystery and vessels are urged not to anchor there, not that anyone is ever very likely to.

THE NEEDLES

Passage through the Needles, often called threading the Needles, is possible for shallow drafted craft at most states of the tide in quiet sea conditions. Further details will be found in *Wight Hazards*.

Passage around the Needles lighthouse is made perilous by the presence of a submerged wreck that causes serious damage to any number of small vessels every year.

The 3,874 ton ship *SS Varvassi* went aground in clear weather at 0700 on 5th January 1947. Before long she

54

The *Varvassi* wreck in the summer of 1947.

broke up and her cargo of strong wine and oranges appeared on nearby beaches: a welcome event at a time of post-war shortages. The remains are positioned as shown on the chart, but her hull has almost entirely fragmented and rusted away leaving only the hefty pieces of her propulsion machinery intact (Plate 55). Of those that are a danger, the most inshore are two squat Scotch boilers that sit on their ends like twin cooking pots. The boilers, which are nearly filled with shingle, are about four metres in diameter and have a vertical dimension of roughly 2.5m.

55

An overhead view of the Needles showing Goose Rock and the four dangerous hunks of wreckage further offshore. Note the tide race running between the inner boiler of the wreck and Goose Rock.

They have large holes in the end plates at the top. Nearly in line to seaward lie the remains of the *Varvassi's* reciprocating steam engine, and a little further out the ship's stern and propeller shaft. Some hull structure lies in deeper water to the west as well as her propeller, which is cast iron and therefore not worth salvaging. The most inshore boiler is 100m from the base of the lighthouse, and both of the boilers are just exposed at chart datum. The engine and the stern tube have a least depth of 0.5m and 0.7m respectively in a surrounding depth of 2.8m. These dangerous remnants of the wreck lie in the line of the Needles on a NNE/SSW heading and are well set in the chalk.

It is possible to venture between the wreck and the lighthouse but such a course, with the nearly sheer-sided Goose Rock (Plate 56) to the north-west of the lighthouse on the one hand and solid boilerplate on the other cannot be recommended. During the Round the Island Race of 2007 two yachts struck rusty steel between the boilers and rocks, probably remnants of *Varvassi's* hull. Minimum depth found within this passage is probably about 2.4m at chart datum. Deeper water, up to 3m at chart datum, can be found on the lighthouse side but the seabed is uneven. A vessel approaching from Alum Bay, and intending to use

56

A yacht aground on Goose Rock during the Round the Island Race.

the inshore passage from north to south, should not pass south of a line between the highest point of the middle Needle and the coastguard station until it is judged that Goose Rock has been passed (Plate 57). Likewise when going from south to north a vessel should not turn to the east towards Alum Bay until north of this transit.

Given patience and good visibility, an obscure but, in the past, fairly reliable transit can be used to find the easternmost boiler. Line up the distant Shingles Elbow Buoy on a bearing of 336°M with the left hand end of an even more distant dark clump of greenery (or something like it) mid way up Hordle Cliff that happens to coincide with a hump of three trees on

57

Goose Rock can be avoided on a course from Alum Bay by keeping the old coastguard station on West High Down in sight when rounding the Needles between the lighthouse and the wreck.

the skyline. Clearly the Elbow Buoy will move with the tidal stream and no reliance at all should be put on this transit for avoiding the wreck.

Various schemes have been proposed to deal with the dangerous parts of the wreck, but so far have been found to be too costly or impractical to implement. Apparently there are three bulging files at Trinity House with impassioned calls for action, but it is Trinity House policy to mark only hazards in passages used for general navigation. A plan for the establishment of a post, funded by the Crown Estate Commissioners, to mark the west end of the wreck is on hold.

From a marine archaeologist's point of view there are two interesting protected wrecks close to the Needles. One of these is a 44-gun warship, *HMS Assurance*, built in 1747 at Heather Yard, Bursledon and wrecked on Goose Rock in 1753 whilst carrying home the retiring governor of Jamaica. The other is another warship, a frigate of 38 guns called *HMS Pomone*. She was built on the river Medway in 1805 and was lost in 1811 after hitting a rock off the Needles on her way into the Solent at night. The port bow section of the *Pomone* has been recently identified lying in Alum Bay. Artefacts can be seen at the naval museum beside *HMS Victory* at Portsmouth.

NEEDLES CHANNEL

Accidents are only too common at the entrance to the Needles Channel. Vessels can easily be caught out by an abrupt change from a regular Channel sea, or from the gentle waters of the Solent to large, steep, breaking seas. In unsettled weather the prudent outward-bound seaman will have secured his vessel properly for sea, have his crew equipped with oilskins, sea boots, lifejackets, safety harnesses and seasick pills, and will be carrying a sensible amount of sail before Hurst Castle is abeam. Inward bound, sensible seafarers will take the same precautions and will be watching carefully to avoid areas where waves are breaking, and that the cross tide is not carrying their vessel towards The Shingles Bank. In severe weather wise mariners will be prepared to avoid the Needles Channel altogether. One alternative is the North Channel, which is sheltered from the full force of the swell by the Shingles Bank. Invariably the seas are calmer in the North Channel, and there is the benefit of a favourable eddy when the main Solent tidal stream is ebbing. In rough weather the North Channel is generally to be preferred, though use of this passage demands that one has to round up towards the wind just short of a lee shore. Should anything go wrong at this juncture a vessel could soon drift onto Hurst Spit. Thus in a really extreme westerly gale there is a strong case for approaching the Solent via Spithead or staying at sea until the weather moderates.

THE SHINGLES

Ancient maps show rock pinnacles appearing above the surrounding level of the Shingles Bank but, if they ever did exist, they have long since gone. Nowadays there is no danger of hitting a rock on the Shingles Bank (Plate 58) and one may even sail over The Shingles at high water on a calm day, when the eerie noise of loose shingle in motion may sometimes be heard. Nevertheless embarrassing encounters with the Shingles have occurred at the start of more than one Round the World Race, when the excitement of the occasion and proximity of many spectator craft may have confused the competitors. Even shallow-draft craft should allow a good margin for unexpected humps that can be formed by gales or the tide. Fifty years ago the Shingles banks appeared more frequently at low water than they do now, though remarkable gravel islands showing about two metres at high water do still emerge from time to time. There is one shown on the

58 (above)

Shingles banks often appear at low water spring tides, but not always in the same place.

59 (right)

Gravel islands form from time to time on the Shingles and show well above sea level at high water.

Admiralty chart of 1921 off Elbow Buoy, one appeared during World War II, another appeared for two months in the spring of 1988 off Elbow Buoy again, another off the Mid Shingles Buoy in early 1990 (Plate 59), and another in the early spring of 2000 and yet again in 2001. It seems that these banks form after a prolonged series of westerly gales.

On the ebb, there is a strong west-going cross-tidal flow on the north side of the Needles Channel causing craft to be set onto the Shingles Bank (Plate 60). Conversely the flood tidal

60 (above)

An 8.5m (28ft) yacht aground on the Shingles one mile west of the Mid Shingles Buoy on the windy day of 26 May 1996. Photograph by Kevin Smith from the Lymington inshore lifeboat crew.

flow will carry craft onto the bank on the North Channel side.

In addition to the shoals, when passing over or close to the Shingles one should look out for breaking seas. Even if only the slightest swell is running, ugly waves can appear as if from nowhere to capsize even quite sizeable vessels. According to the Needles Lighthouse keepers of yore, waves over the Shingles tend to break more on the flood tide than the ebb. At the outer end of the Needles Channel in a southwesterly gale ferocious breaking waves can extend from the Shingles towards the Bridge Buoy, leaving nowhere completely safe. Nevertheless the calmest water will usually be found close to either side of the Bridge Buoy, though in moderate conditions some prefer to take a course half way between the Bridge Buoy and the Needles Lighthouse where three or four vicious seas may be experienced, but that will be all. Fishermen often use the patch of calmer water just west from the *Varvassi* wreck on the way to and from the open sea.

There is a recently-found wreck 0.5m below chart datum on the northeast tip of the Shingles Bank. The survey vessel *Proud Sea Horse* hit it whilst surveying in October 1994, and it is now shown on the chart.

HURST POINT TO LYMINGTON – HURST SPIT

Hurst Spit is a curious hook-shaped shingle formation jutting 1.2 miles out from the Hampshire shore into the Solent towards the Isle of Wight (Plate 61). The constriction to the tidal flow caused by Hurst Spit creates very strong tidal streams, circular areas of flat sea caused by up welling water and unusual spiky waves.

Hurst Castle, located on the tip of Hurst, was one of many anti-invasion coastal fortresses built by Henry VIII, using the proceeds from the dissolution of the monasteries. Some of the stone is said to have come from Beaulieu Abbey. The original castle was completed in 1544, but the structure is largely hidden from seaward by two massive wing batteries, which were constructed between 1861 and 1879 to deter hostile French ships from entering the Solent. The shells from the 38-ton rifled muzzle-loading guns were said to have been able to penetrate wrought iron of great thickness. The dark squares of the batteries are due to heavy iron shields that were an important defensive feature of the fortifications. None of the mighty nineteenth century Solent defences was ever put to the test.

King Charles I was imprisoned

61

Hurst peninsula.

briefly in Hurst Castle in December 1648 prior to his trial and execution in 1649. Subsequently the castle was designated as a prison for those convicted of fostering the growth of Popery. A priest named Father Paul Atkinson suffered this fate in 1700 and was to remain in Hurst Castle for the rest of his life. A small community lived at Hurst at one time: enough people including the soldiers from the battery to support three inns, the Shipwrights Arms, the New Inn and the Castle Inn.

As far as yachtsmen are concerned Hurst is also famous for its well-named 'Trap' (Plate 62). This sand spit sticks 60m out into the channel opposite the westernmost casemate black iron shield of the eastern wing battery, and gives little warning on an echo sounder. In fact the depth drops nearly 4m between off the south bastion of the old castle and off the second black casemate shield to the east. Aerial photographs taken since 1983 show that The Trap, as it is usually known, varies quite considerably in height and extent. When entering the Solent against an ebb tide and making use of the eddy on the west side of Hurst Beach, it is advisable to head decisively into deeper water before the circular-looking Henry VIII castle, the so-called Round Fort, which can just be seen above the level of the wing batteries, is on the beam

6

62 (above)

Looking north at the tip of Hurst Point. The sand bar, aptly named The Trap, is quite evident just east of the Round Fort.

63 (right)

The south bastion of the Round Fort on the left and the first 'black window' to the right of the Hurst lighthouse.

(Plate 63). Those who have been stuck on The Trap report that the ebb tide holds back the Channel swell, which then reappears on the flood tide with startling force (Plate 64). This was more than one yacht's keelbolts could survive, so she capsized and was lost. Past The Trap, heading east, one is in deeper water again close to the south-east tip of Hurst Spit.

64 (right)

A yacht aground on The Trap.

KEYHAVEN

There is noticeable erosion of the shoreline on both sides of the Hurst Spit, except at the south side of the Keyhaven River mouth where the spit called North Point has extended in past years. The whole of the western side of Hurst Beach is suffering from this erosion, and after the spit was temporarily breached in a storm, vastly expensive reinforcement work was completed.

After closing on the Hampshire shore, a sounding can be picked up and followed past Hurst Spit and Pennington towards the Lymington River. Navigators of large deep-drafted yachts will notice that the seabed shelves rapidly once Hurst High Light is past the beam.

To enter Keyhaven, pick up the leading marks on a bearing of 283°M. These are red and white posts on the marsh (the red part being fluorescent) and lead to the port and starboard hand entrance buoys. Then turn to port when the first green channel mark comes in sight and leave the red buoy off North Point, marking a central bank, to port (Plate 65). This is the shallowest part of the channel and has less than a metre at an extreme spring low tide.

Facilities at Keyhaven have been much improved of late. It is now possible to go alongside anywhere on the quay as the adjoining seabed has

Looking east over Keyhaven entrance. The entrance of Hawkers Lake is towards the top left hand corner of the photo with Stivers Lake beyond.

66

Keyhaven Lake on the left, Hawkers Lake on the right.

recently been dredged deeper and flatter. Depth alongside at high water springs is 2.3m. On the north side of the quay there is now a scrubbing grid and an additional slipway (Plate 66). A very high spring tide causes the whole quay area to flood. The river warden's phone number is 01590645695.

In 2001, a red and black IALA-type buoy was laid in the approach to Hawker's Lake to mark the steep spit on the port side. On the way up Hawkers Lake a sand bar has developed at the entrance to Iley Lake, to be found opposite a green 4 knot speed restriction notice (Plate 67). Many deeper-keeled boats will only be able to cross the sand bar near high water, if at all.

67 (above)

The 4k speed restriction notice in Hawkers Lake not only marks the entrance of Iley Lake but also marks the presence of a sand bar.

Iley Lake has gradually widened and deepened over the years and, at high water, makes a delightful passageway for dinghies connecting, as it does, Hawkers and Stivers Lakes (Plate 68). Iley Lake is often now called Stivers Lake though, strictly speaking,

lley Lake is navigable by small craft at high water. It leads out into the Solent through Stivers Lake.

Stivers Lake covers just the entrance to the east of Hawker's Lake. The lone rock shown on old charts off Hawker's Lake does not exist.

Colonel Peter Hawker, the author's great-great-great grandfather, was a celebrated Keyhaven 19th century sportsman. As a young lieutenant he became the hero of the Douro action in 1809 whilst serving under Wellington in the Peninsular War. Later he was invalided from the army after being seriously wounded at the battle of Talavera. Though his injuries were to trouble him for the rest of his life, he spent much of his time in demonstrating how one could bring to the oven some of the great abundance of wild-fowl to be found on the marshes, an extremely popular accomplishment before the days of supermarkets. He also took command of Keyhaven emergencies, such as the breaching of the sea wall, besides supervising and paying for Hawker's Lake, the useful short cut into Keyhaven named after him.

Nowadays there probably are not so many wildfowl but, in winter, large flocks of brent geese arrive and a small colony of Slavonian grebes forms. Very cold weather brings longtailed ducks, mergansers and the occasional goosander and smew. In summer one may be lucky enough to spot little terns and Dartford warblers whilst little egrets have become common since 1989.

On both sides of Pennington sewer beacon, particularly to the east, the bottom is lumpy to the extent of half a metre. At low water vessels drawing more than a metre can get caught out along this shore, as shoal water extends out beyond the line of the Pennington sewer beacon and Jack in the Basket. In particular, there is a ridge of shingle running parallel to the shore south east of the Pennington sewer post with less than half a metre over it at chart datum. Inshore of this bank the depth can be up to 1.6m deeper (Fig 1) which can lead to a false sense of security. The shoal area is opposite the easternmost bungalow on the Hampshire shore and roughly in line with Colten Buoy and the big power station chimney at Fawley. Alternatively it lies on a line when the Hurst fortifications are open their own width clear of the Needles.

The marshes off Keyhaven and Lymington are retreating at the rate of 4-5 metres per year due to natural erosion and the dieback of spartina grasses. The spartina grass only appeared around the turn of the last century and there is no obvious reason for its decline. Other plants such as sea purslane and sea lavender are appearing to take the place of the spartina grasses but these plants like a greater height above sea level to propagate, and are not likely to affect the rate of erosion very much. The extent of the marshes in 1781 can be seen in Fig 2

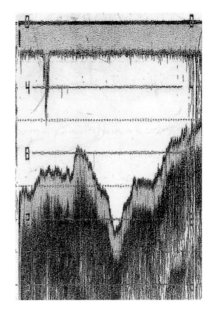

Fig 1

A south-north sounding run to the east of Pennington sewer post showing the shingle ridge. The soundings are in feet.

but, in spite of the marked reduction since, there are still channels that can provide an enjoyable passage for dinghies at high tide. Channels are tending to widen due to the erosion and, in doing so, become navigable by very small boats.

At low water, in addition to the shingle, there are odd places where a dark spongy substance can be seen on the shore between Hurst and Lymington. This comes from submerged peat beds such as may also be found at low water along the shore around Yarmouth. In addition to the peat beds, close inspection of the

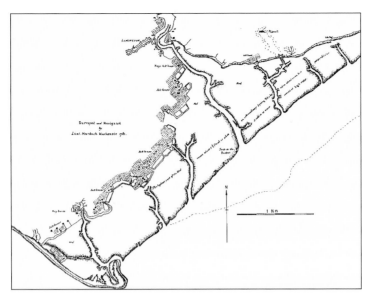

Fig 2

The extent of the marshes off Keyhaven and
Lymington in 1781.

beach gravel at Pennington will show
that some of it is common flint stone,
as might be expected, and some of it is
smoothly-rounded wood from ancient
forest which at one time commonly
grew to the water's edge along the whole
south coast of England. The peat beds
and the forest were submerged when the
sea level rose 12m between 6000 and
3000 years ago. It is a curious fact that
coastal sediment has excellent preserva-
tive qualities and, for example, recently
exposed Solent pine tree roots have
been carbon dated back to 6000 BC.

The 1.5m Pennington sewer pipe
laid in 1980 is in a trench and is not a
hazard. Its effluent is much improved
after a long-overdue treatment plant

was brought into use at the end of
1995. The only part that protrudes
above the seabed is the T-piece dif-
fuser, which is 2m above pipe level,
and is located 6m inshore of the sewer
boom. The two outer sections of the
old pipe were never removed, so it is
said, and still lie to the north of the
sewer post, but in deep enough water
to present little risk to passing craft.

The sea wall between Lymington
and Keyhaven was renovated at great
expense between 1990 and 1994 (Plate
69) following the deterioration of the
previous wall, which was reputed to
have been built by French prisoners of
the Napoleonic War. Behind the wall
there is still evidence of Lymington's
saltpans, that for six hundred years
were the principal source of the

69

Middle Island, Oxey Lake and Norrey Lake at high water, looking towards Lymington.

nation's salt. Oxey Dock, the back end of the recess in the old wall opposite Oxey Lake, can still be seen. This was where barges took the ground to disembark Kentish coal used in the dehydration process, before reloading with salt for distribution and sale elsewhere. Mounds can also be seen inside the sea wall on which windmills were built to pump the salt water from the saltpans to the boiling houses.

The sewer pipe of Oxey, half a mile to the east, was mostly removed when the present Pennington sewer outfall was constructed, except for a section close to the island between Oxey and Norrey Lakes (Plate 70). Since the removal of the pipe, Oxey Lake and Narrow Mark channels leading to the Lymington River through Crooked Lake, or to the Yacht Haven, have become useful to small craft at high water (Plate 71). As a matter of interest rather than concern, during World War II a German bomb is said to have landed in the mud on the south side of Crooked Lake without exploding. In addition, not far away, a Gannet aircraft crash-landed on Shell Island in the 1950s. It was winched to a lighter in the river, which accounts for the straight grooves in the marsh, which can still be seen from the upper passenger deck of the Lymington-Yarmouth ferry. On the subject of these ferries, one should mention that though, at low water, they take up much of the channel in the Lymington River, their Voith Schneider propellers make them highly manoeuvrable even when stationary. Unlike shipping and ferries in the more congested area between Cowes and the Hamble, they are seldom a problem to smaller craft in the open Solent.

70 (above)

Oxey and Norrey Lake at low water.

71 (below)

Shell Island in the foreground, and the Oxey Lake, Norrey Lake and Crooked Lake channels, which enable shallow drafted boats to reach the Lymington Yacht Haven at high water without use of the Lymington River fairway.

LYMINGTON TO THORNS BEACH

Lymington is a well-sheltered and popular harbour but, due to the controversial construction of a causeway over the river in 1731 by a merchant navy captain, Captain Cross, silting tends to occur through loss of scouring effect. This is ameliorated by the scouring effect of the ferries, which keep the channel depth constant over the part they use. However the Lymington River is not as deep as the Hamble River, though it is easier to enter than the Beaulieu River. Vessels with drafts of over 1.8m may have difficulties in the lower part of the Lymington River at extreme low water spring tides, and will definitely have a problem in reaching the town quay (Plate 72).

In November 1977 the unlit Lymington Spit Buoy was removed, but replaced by the lit Lymington Banks buoy in 2006. The bank lies 100m south and 400m southeast from the Royal Lymington Yacht Club starting platform which, incidentally, is not lit and it is possible to run aground here at low water when approaching the Royal Lymington Yacht Club line to the south of the platform. Between the starting platform and Tanners Lake the mud banks vary in height by at least half a metre and in random manner confounding even the locals, but at

72

The Lymington River.

73 (above)

At high water Pylewell Lake allows a pretty and sheltered way out from Lymington to the east.

74 (left)

Freshwater Lake provides a continuation from Pylewell Lake for very shallow drafted boats. Note The Cut in the centre foreground.

half tide or more one can make a useful hitch into Pylewell Lake, and work close to the bank at high water.

Pylewell Creek dries out, but at high water it provides a useful and lovely short cut for small craft, with a maximum depth of about 2m at springs (Plate 73). One can either come out into the Solent or take another rather shallower creek, called Freshwater Lake that leads east from Pylewell Lake, coming out into the Solent opposite Tanners Lane via a manmade channel called The Cut (Plate 74). The main Freshwater Lake channel is impossibly narrow and

75 (above)

Freshwater Lake at low tide.

76 (right)

A shallow channel, where bird life prospers, runs between Tanners Lake and Pitts Deep Lake.

there is no more than a metre elsewhere at high water (Plate 75). East of Tanners Lake there is another slightly deeper inland waterway, emerging at Pitts Deep (Plate 76).

To seaward of Pitts Deep, at three metres depth, there is a one-metre high soft clay peat-covered mini cliff running approximately parallel to the shore. At the base of this small cliff the seabed changes from clay to peat-covered shingle. Off the saltings at Sowley (Plate 77) the sand comes far out and changes appreciably from year to year.

To the east, the metal posts of the wartime barrier off Durns Point,

77 (above)
Sowley sand bank.

78 (left)
The Sowley boom. Except for the light platform, all the outer posts have fallen over in the past ten years.

marked as 'obstruction' on the chart and often called the Sowley Boom, are falling over with age (Plate 78). In 2001 Army divers established that there are twelve submerged stumps proud of the seabed between the light platform and the nearest visible inshore post. The stumps vary between 1m and 3m in height. It is, therefore, wiser to go round the boom rather than though the gap. Plans to remove the boom have been postponed indefinitely for elaborate environmental reasons. It was feared that removal of the boom would cause sudden changes in currents and sedimentation, leading to

79

Looking north at Park Shore bank.

major changes in the shape of the shoreline as far as the Beaulieu River. Whether it has anything to do with the remaining barrier or not, an inshore bank is growing immediately to the east of the posts with a spit lying nearly parallel to the line of the boom. The spit starts to dry not long after high water.

The chart shows an area where anchoring and trawling is prohibited between the old booms off Durns and Hamstead Point. This is another legacy from the Second World War when a steel wire boom was positioned between the two barriers as a defence against hostile submarines. There was also a controlled minefield there and some sort of range. No doubt obstructions such as sinkers and wire cable

were left on the seabed when the boom was removed at the end of the war, which would account for the prohibition. Local trawler fishermen say that the only obstruction known to be in existence is a concrete block in deep water opposite the northerly barrier, so it is possible that not much else remains on the seabed. An anchor, on the other hand, is more likely to snag buried cables than a trawl, so it would be wise to continue to heed the restriction.

Beyond the barrier, the bottom is moderately shelving up to the treacherous Park Shore shingle banks (Plate 79). The first of these is south of the white house at Thorns Beach. There follows a deceptive indentation followed by sudden shoals that often catch the

80

Looking northeast over the Park Shore banks. Note the Beaulieu mudflats beyond and the inlet opposite Lord Montague's beach house.

068°M to give a useful line. Unfortunately there will be times when neither the Purbeck Hills nor the chalk pit can be seen and, in this event, keep outside the transit of the eastern of the two beach houses and the Fawley Power Station chimney.

THE LEPE BANK

A large stretch of sand and mud, extending well out into the Solent and called the Lepe Bank, lies off the old coastguard cottages at Needs Ore Point. At high water one can pass over it, but at other times it presents a large but fairly flat obstacle. An awkward channel in the form of a dogleg lies between Lepe Bank and the shore, where there is about 0.5m more water than immediately to seaward.

There is a slight lip on the east side of Lepe Bank at right angles to the shore that shows up from the air (Plate 81). When approaching the coastguard cottages from the east, look for the roof of the Beaulieu River Sailing Club. When opposite this building a small reduction in depth, perhaps 0.2m may be apparent.

THE BEAULIEU SPIT

The Beaulieu Spit extends from Needs Ore Point to the Beaulieu River entrance. The short cut at Needs Ore

unwary (Plate 80). On the west side of this bank there lies at SSW/NNE a 20m long metal pipe of 0.3m diameter, sometimes marked with a plastic float, and which dries at low water springs. A fence extending 150m into the sea marks the eastern limit of the Park Shore banks. A good line to give a clearing transit is not easy to find. To the west, the transit between the outermost structure of Durns Point barrier in line with the highest point on the Purbeck Hills on 255°M will serve in good visibility. To the east, the 'oil rig' structure at Stansore Point has been removed leaving only the right hand edge of the Paulsgrove Chalk Pit at Portsdown Hill on a bearing of

7

81

Looking east towards Stansore Point. The lip on the east side of Lepe Bank can just be seen in the foreground as well as the east end of the indistinct and tortuous inner passage.

82

Looking northwest to Needs Ore Point and to the causeway blocking off the Swatchway (or Bulls Run). The channel leading to Exbury River quay can be seen on the extreme right. Note that the Beaulieu Spit mudbanks in the foreground are uneven.

Point, known as the Swatchway or Bulls Run, was closed in 1986 to protect Gull Island against continuing erosion, which was expected to affect Exbury marshes and the anchorage in the first reach of the river (Plate 82). It was stated that the channel could be reopened if the closure was to prove ineffective, but the erosion is now said to be much less severe. To seaward of Gull Island the bottom is slightly lumpy and it is wise to allow a margin of half a metre or so on the depth sounder.

BEAULIEU RIVER

The banks on the east side of the Beaulieu River entrance can be approached with the aid of an echo sounder. The splendid 8m high white

Millennium Beacon established in July 2000 now houses the leading light, (Plate 83). Of course few yachts can enter the Beaulieu River at all states of the tide as the least depth at the entrance is only 0.8m but, that said, the lower reaches are deep and it is a very beautiful river, worthy of exploration (Plate 84). There is a speed limit of 5k.

STANSORE POINT

Some 0.6nm to the east of the dolphin at the Beaulieu River entrance, there is a shingle bank known as Horseshoe Spit coming out from Stansore Point towards the Lepe Spit Buoy (Plate 85). This buoy was established in May

83 (above)

The Beaulieu River millennium beacon.

84 (below)

The Beaulieu River with Bucklers Hard in the centre of the photo.

1988 when the last of the Southern Electric beacons was removed. At high water spring tides small yachts will pass over Horseshoe Spit (Plate 86), but at other times it is advisable to stay outside the buoy. Keen racing crews may wish to identify some mark ashore when the tidal height just allows their boat to cross the spit.

At high water springs one can

85 (left)

Horseshoe Spit off Stansore point at low water.

86 (below)

Horseshoe Spit at half tide. Lepe Spit Buoy can be seen on the left.

87

An exposed steel pipe seen from sea level. These pipes may have been the cause of several heavy groundings.

Spit, managed to escape it. This spit may be the obstruction shown on the chart reported in 1988 as 'position approximate'.

Many Isle of Wight service pipes and cables run from Stansore Point along the seabed to Egypt Point, Gurnard and Thorness Bays. Though the pipes are well buried in the seabed inshore, they are largely exposed further offshore so the prohibited anchorage area exists for good reason. Every year anchors foul the cables. For example, in 1992 there were two incidents where the steel wire armour of a power cable was sufficiently damaged to cause the cooling oil to leak out. In one incident the damage was done by a motor cruiser's anchor, which the owner did not want to lose. He requested help and in doing so revealed his identity. Later he was presented with a bill for the damage to the cable, which would probably have paid for hundreds of anchors. In the other incident, which occurred in shallow water on the east side of Stansore Point, it seemed likely that a yacht's keel had caused the problem. In addition to the three 132KV power cables of 14 cm diameter, there are also three steel gas pipes of 10mm wall thickness and 0.3m external diameter, including the concrete coating. There are two water pipes and three telephone cables. Finally there

approach the shore closely to the east of Stansore Point, and pass close to or even between the two dolphins marked on the chart. However the eastern side of the shingle bank at Stansore Point can vary quite markedly, and a number of heavy groundings occurred during the 1992 Cowes Week on a spit, which has built up around an apparently redundant steel pipe (Plate 87). It is one of the areas where yachts should tack when there is still at least two metres under the keel. Two Sigma 38s, *Yeoman XXVIII* and *Profit*, and an IMC yacht called *Highlander* were amongst those that went aground whilst on a southerly course. Others in their class on the same tack, but further inshore towards Horseshoe

are other, probably redundant, pipes that appear in places on the surface of the shingle at extreme low water spring tides. These are probably the ones that caused the trouble in the 1992 Cowes Week. One runs towards Egypt Point and the other lies approximately east/west. One speculates that they may have been Solo pipes that led over to Thorness Bay. (see page 22)

STANSWOOD BAY

To the east of Stansore Point, in Stanswood Bay, the shore is gently shelving and an echo sounder gives adequate guidance when working in to avoid a contrary tide. A west-going eddy may be found close to the beach when the main stream is flooding strongly. If very close in near high water, when taking advantage of the eddy, one will need to watch out for the groynes. The tide gauge shown on the chart has gone and is not likely to be replaced.

During World War II numerous sections of Mulberry harbour were constructed at the top of the western beach, which accounts for its flat appearance. There are oyster beds in Stanswood Bay that are harvested periodically by a large number of fishing boats belonging to the 'Oyster Cooperative'. These boats tow twin dredges and may make unexpected manoeuvres.

The dark-looking rectangular structure inshore of Bourne Gap Buoy, with tunnels leading to it, is the cooling water outlet from Fawley Power Station. It is lit and there are no particular obstructions surrounding it other than what can be seen. However there is some low profile junk around on the seabed, so it is not a good place to anchor. To the northwest, on the beach opposite the Fawley cooling water outlet, there is an outfall marked by a bent post at the shore end. The pipe is 0.3m in diameter and rises about the same amount clear of the seabed in places (Plate 88).

There is public access to the Stanswood Bay beach between low and high water marks, but severe erosion has affected the cliff face and falling trees are quite common.

88

The outfall to the north of Stanswood Bay. Nothing marks the end of the pipe.

CALSHOT

Many years ago Calshot used to be an island, distinguished by its Henry VIII fort. Nowadays the causeway beach is popular with windsurfers, water skiers, and dinghy sailors. The spit running southeastwards from the causeway is an obvious trap for those unfamiliar with the Solent as it extends well out from the shore (Plate 89), and also because many small craft cross it at high water (Plate 90). One can work out routes for cutting the corner for a given draft and state of the tide, but if in doubt stay out. At low water one may need to take a course close to the Calshot side of the port hand channel navigation buoys in order to leave the main fairway clear for shipping.

89 (left)

Calshot Spit at low water, looking north.

90 (below)

Calshot Spit near high water.

THE BRAMBLES

The Bramble Bank is shaped like an arrowhead pointing southwest. It is composed of blue clay covered by gravel and fine sand (Plate 91). West Knoll Buoy and the Brambles Post mark the Brambles adequately, but it is easy to misjudge the position of the bank or simply forget that it is there, and from time to time yachts are stranded on it for all to see. Unless the tide is high enough to pass over the Bramble Bank, particular care is necessary to leave West Knoll to starboard when on a course from the west Solent towards Clipper Buoy. When passing to the west of the Brambles Bank, the twin chimneys of the Cowes generating station provide a useful transit. As long as there is a gap between the two chimneys on a bearing of about 178°M there is about 1.5m depth at chart datum but, as the Brambles Bank is moving very slowly to the west, this transit should be used with caution. The Bramble Bank Post transmits weather information that can be obtained on the *www.scra.org.uk* website. West Knoll Buoy is now lit, characteristic fl.yellow.2.5s, with the object of keeping small craft out of the main fairway.

Uffa Fox, and many others since, have played cricket on the bank at low water spring tide (Plate 92) but the

91

The Brambles, looking south towards Cowes. The post is to the left of the bank.

92

A cricket match between the Royal Southern Yacht Club and the Island Sailing Club in September 2000. On this occasion it was the Royal Southern's turn to win. Note that the bank shelves most steeply on the south side.

surface undulates with large puddles in between, which does not provide an entirely satisfactory pitch, and runs are hard to make.

East Knoll Bank does not show up strongly on the chart and can be an embarrassment to deep-drafted yachts at low tide, as can another large shallow area with a charted depth of less than one metre extending one and a half miles to the east of the Bramble Bank. As a relatively new arrival in the Solent, this bank has no official name. Unofficially it is sometimes called the Limit Bank, as it happens to lie at the limit of the Ports of Southampton and

Portsmouth. At one low water in 1985 a British Admiral's Cup Team practice race had to be abandoned after most of the fleet had gone aground here.

Having invited due caution regarding the Bramble and adjoining banks, one should mention that the strength of the tide can be markedly weaker over these shallow areas. When there is sufficient depth to do so, this can be used to advantage when the tide is foul.

HAMBLE RIVER TO BROWNDOWN POINT

The shore from the Hamble River (Plate 93) to just before Titchfield Haven, officially also known as Hill Head Harbour, is generally gently shelving muddy sand that dries out some way from the shore at low water. The exception is a small patch of stones some 100m west of Brownwich Lane.

A prominent hard shell and shingle spit called Rainbow Bar lies to the west of Hill Head Harbour. It is marked with a discoloured – once black and yellow – post with a large guanoed – once yellow – topmark with seven spikes like a three-dimensional star, popular as a drying out perch for cormorants (Plate 94).

Old maps show Hill Head as Hell Head for some reason. Another point of historical interest is that the Meon

93 (above)

Exposed shingle banks and mudflats at the entrance of the Hamble River.

94 (below)

Rainbow Bar looking northwest. The post may just be seen off the tip.

Hill Head Harbour and the Titchfield Haven nature reserve.

River at one time allowed vessels to reach the important trading centre of Titchfield from the sea. In the early 17th Century a sea wall was constructed across the river mouth and a narrow canal was built for barges, with lock gates at the seaward end. It was an ambitious undertaking and is said not to have been popular with the inhabitants of Titchfield. The canal was completed and initially worked well but kept being blocked by shingle much as the river channel had been. Use of the canal was discontinued altogether by the end of the 19th Century. The annual Titchfield carnival still celebrates the burning of an effigy of Henry, Third Earl of Southampton who was the owner of the land beside the Meon River and the perpetrator of the canal scheme. The Earl does not entirely deserve this indignity for, apart from patronising William Shakespeare, he undertook a large number of good works locally and, far from being a tyrant, he seems to have tried to be a major benefactor. Even his canal scheme worked better than the river, which had been steadily silting up.

Visitors are welcome in the harbour (Plate 95) and equally welcome at the Hill Head Sailing Club, which administers the harbour.

96

The shore dries out some way from Hill Head Harbour at low water springs.

The local sailing boats tend to be no more than 7m (22ft) and have bilge keels or a centreplate, though up to 7.5m (25ft) in length is allowed. The practical limit for visiting craft is about 9m (29.5ft) length and 1.5m draft, but larger craft do visit from time to time. If there is room, it is best for visitors to berth alongside the wall where the Meon enters. A post bearing an orange buoy of diameter 45cm (18in) marks the groyne on the port side of the entrance. In addition to the sailing club, the adjoining nature reserve provides another attraction. Rare birds such as bearded tits and

Cetti's warblers can be seen and heard all year round, while wild flowers such as marsh mallow, summer snowflake and slender bird's foot trefoil (*lotus angustissimus*) can be found.

The deepest water is not easy to find in the approaches. Generally the shingle seabed is quite flat, but mounds develop at random (Plate 96). Heavy rain increases the river flow and produces a straight run into the harbour but thereafter meanders develop. The best advice is to feel the way in on a rising tide on a line between All Saints, the tall church spire on the skyline at Ryde, and the harbour entrance: a course of 330°M.

Hill Head Harbour marks the

The banks off Hill Head. Knights Bank is half way down the picture.

westernmost limit of the Dockyard Port of Portsmouth. This area, which extends from Old Castle Point in the southwest to Eastney, Shanklin and almost to the Nab Tower to the east, comes under the jurisdiction of the Queen's Harbourmaster, Portsmouth. There is a speed limit in his area of 10k within 914m (1000 yards) of the shore and there is a byelaw for the protection of bathers off Hill Head.

A point of interest is that the Hill Head Sailing Club used to start their races from an old boatyard, which operated from boatsheds below the site of the present Osborne View Hotel. Some of the wood used to build the boatyard is said to have come from duckboards from the Bathing Pier at Osborne Bay after a gale in the 1930's.

The shallow coastline to the southeast of Hill Head Harbour dries out some way and should not be approached closely at low water (Plate 97). There is a shallow bank, called Knight's Bank, about 100m to the east of the Osborne View Hotel, and another shallow bank, locally called Shark Bank, that has grown out to 250m from the shore, adjacent to the water skiing area bounded by unlit yellow buoys. It lies between the west end of the eastern beach huts, which are to be seen where the main road from Stubbington forks left for Lee-on-Solent and right via Sea Lane towards Hill Head, and a groyne to the west (Plate 98). The significance of this spit is that, in an area of gently shelving shingle, sand or mud there is

8

98 (above)

Shark Bank lies between Hill Head and Lee on Solent.

99 (below)

The hovercraft slipway at Lee on Solent.

a 100m patch of rocks dotted about off the spit, some of which dry at spring tides.

Six hundred metres further east the concrete hovercraft slipway will be found at what was *HMS Daedalus*, identifiable by the aircraft hangars behind (Plate 99). The small buoys off the slipway mark a channel for jet skiers out to a designated jet ski area. The slipway extends some 100m into the Solent, but beyond this one can work the shingle beach closely as far as Lee Point (Plate 100), groynes, bathers, dinghies and canoes permitting. Big blocks of raw rock have recently replaced the old wooden groynes, and the posts marking them

100 (above)

The mud and shingle bank off Lee Point looking northwest.

101 (below)

A yacht aground off Lee Point. Note the post with topmark behind.

are not on the ends of the groynes as they used to be. There have been several incidents off this shore involving small craft, particularly racing yachts, and bathers. Another byelaw is in force requiring special care between the extreme western end of the sea wall and promenade at Lee on Solent, all the way to the junction of Dolphin Way with the seawall at the former Royal Naval Hospital at Haslar, for a distance of 805m (880 yards) to seaward.

With the prevailing wind as it is, the coastline between the Hamble and Gilkicker is exposed to the southwest and should be treated with the respect due to any lee shore. At Lee (or locally Elmore) Point there is a mud and sand spit extending 400m out. A green post, not marked on the chart, marks the end of a surface water drain, but the bank continues at least 50m further to seaward of the post (Plate 101). At high water one can work the shore from Lee Point to Stokes Bay (Plate 102) past the massive Browndown double sewer outfall marked by a green buoy. The 1.8m square pipes have been let into a trench with the intention of being deep enough to avoid even an aircraft carrier's anchor. Only the diffusers stick up from the seabed, and with a minimum depth of 11m they are not likely to present a hazard to yachtsmen. Though the

102

Looking southeast from Lee Point to Stokes Bay and Fort Gilkicker.

sewer pipe may be disregarded, caution and close attention to the echo sounder are necessary along this shore at low water. The well-covered wreck 510m to the northeast of the Browndown buoy is the tank landing craft *LCT 1068*, which sank on 6th June 1947, complete with two tanks. Both the landing craft and the tanks have sunk into the sand and divers, it is said, see it best after a southeasterly gale when the sand has been partially swept away. Other seabed objects nearby which have caught trawl nets or racing mark moorings are a steam pinnace 100m to the west of *LCT 1068* and an aircraft engine 620m west of Gilkicker Point. The pinnace

was the patrol vessel for the old torpedo range that once existed off Browndown, until she was accidentally sunk by one of the trial torpedoes. The aircraft engine has twelve cylinders in line and is said to have come from a Dornier bomber.

There is an Army firing range at Browndown, and in about 1974 the designer of a Vosper Thorneycroft hovercraft undergoing trials on the Solent was wounded in the arm by a wayward bullet at a time when schoolboys were using a rifle range. However the three 600 yard rifle ranges were closed down not long afterwards and there is now only an enclosed 25m range. The beach to the east of Lee Point is used about once a month for amphibious landings, the navy uses the area for firing flares as part of sea survival training and the army use the area for blowing up unexploded ordnance. The range area is rich in shingle plants, amongst which are geraniums called little robin and campions called Nottingham catchfly. Moreover a rare beetle called the blood-headed weevil can also be found there.

STOKES BAY TO PORTSMOUTH HARBOUR

Stokes Bay is a popular haunt for bathers, wind surfers and fishermen, and so it may not be wise to go in too close. In addition to the byelaws requiring special care to be taken when within 805m (880 yards) of the shore, the Stokes Bay Sailing Club has laid a line of ten yellow buoys at 50m from the shore between the outfall at the west corner of Stokes Bay, in position 50° 47.1'N 001°10.0'W, and the Gosport Inshore Rescue Services Headquarters, in position 50°46.7'N 001°08.9'W. No passing vessel is allowed inside this line of yellow buoys. A green post marks an outfall pipe at the west corner of the bay. Furthermore it serves to indicate a growing ridge of gravel deposited by the adjacent outlet for the river Alver (Plate 103) that has virtually covered the whole pipe. Another green post has been placed about half way along the bay – more or less opposite the Alverbank Hotel – on the end of a

103

The gravel bank and exposed drain pipe at the west end of Stokes Bay, marked by a green post.

short drainpipe.

Stokes Bay has two notable offshore obstructions. There is a dangerous wreck 520m from the beach, opposite the Stokes Bay Sailing Club, of charted depth 0.9m, thought to be part of the lighter *Duddon* that sank in 1924. If one is working soundings up the shore, one should be north of a line between Gilkicker Point and Horse Sand Fort to be clear of this wreck. There are no plans to mark it. Apart from this and the byelaw, one can work the soundings all the way round the bay, taking care to keep to seaward of a yellow conical buoy where an old pier used to be (Plate 104). This marks the other notable obstruction,

which is the final remnant of a pier that was once served by a railway line. Lumps of concrete, greenheart, and metal posts protrude half a metre or more above the seabed and four or five can be seen at low water spring tides. To avoid all these hazards when making for the slipway just to the west of the yellow conical Pier Buoy, one needs to head for the red doors marked 'Gosport and Fareham Inshore Rescue' ensuring that one is to the west of a line extending from the lifeboat building's eastern wall, (i.e. if any of this wall is visible on the Gilkicker side, one is in danger of hitting something). Both Stokes Bay slipways have a lip at their lower end, which makes for serious difficulties with boat trailers at low water springs.

Though the area between the yellow buoy and Gilkicker is well sheltered in a northerly wind, vessels anchoring there have been fouling their anchors on a 2.6cm steel cable roughly in the form of a ring, which now seems to be well spread about, causing frequent trouble.

At high water Portsmouth an eastgoing eddy forms up to 150 metres from the shore at the east end of Stokes Bay and continues to run for the next two hours.

When close to Gilkicker Point one has to be careful of fishermen with rod and line, and of the Mussel Patch

104

The remains of the Stokes Bay Pier, marked by a yellow buoy.

Fort Monckton's collection of prominent reinforced concrete blocks are partially visible at low water spring tide.

Shoal round the corner, once said to be good for lobsters. Just off Fort Monckton, the school for budding James Bonds, 600m northeast of Gilkicker, there is quite a collection of reinforced concrete blocks, reminiscent of invasion defences, known locally as the 'Monckton Blocks' (Plate 105). They stand a metre above the seabed, and one or two of them are just exposed at extreme low springs. It is another Solent hazard for which an ordinary echo sounder will not help much (Plate 106).

Once safely past these hazards, the Inner Swashway Channel can be used at high water as a short cut into

106

This white motor cruiser was heading towards Portsmouth at speed, and on rounding Gilkicker Point hit the Monckton Blocks and sank. Photo by Gosport and Fareham Inshore Rescue senior Cox'n Kenneth Pink.

Portsmouth Harbour by vessels less than 20m. Both this passage along the shore and Hamilton Bank are said to be building up with sand owing to the cessation of nearby dredging operations, and there is very little depth at

107

Hamilton Bank awash, with a yacht stranded on its southern end. When a battleship, HMS Nelson, went aground there in 1932 the officers of HMS Dolphin, the overlooking submarine base, jokingly offered the battleship officers honorary membership of their mess 'for the duration of their stay'. The fact that Nelson was on Hamilton also caused some amusement at the time.

low water spring tides.

Spit Sand is cut by the Swash Channel which ferries to the Isle of Wight use at high tide, but beware of the numerous small obstructions between the outer and inner Swash Channels described on the chart, as they are solid blocks of up to 0.9m height. The channel, with a minimum depth of about 2m, lies on a line between the conspicuous war memorial and a block of flats on a bearing of about 050°M. The *Mary Rose* yellow wreck buoy with light characteristic

Fl.Y.5s, is in position about half a mile to the south of Spit Sand Fort. Other associated possibly unlit yellow buoys may be found in the immediate vicinity, and one is asked to keep 300m clear.

Whatever channel is taken to Portsmouth Harbour entrance one should be wary of Hamilton Bank (Plate 107), which often dries out in the summer with the odd small craft on display. Even a battleship once sat out a tide there. A hundred metres south of Fort Blockhouse on the west side of Portsmouth Harbour entrance stands a port hand beacon named BC Outer (Oc.R.15s). Port regulations require this beacon be left to port even when coming from the Inner Swashway. If the tide is ebbing hard

Portsmouth Harbour entrance at near high water.

through the entrance, care should be taken that an incoming vessel is not carried into the main channel.

Entry into Portsmouth Harbour for shipping is controlled by a system of lights displayed at Fort Blockhouse signal station. Vessels under 20m in length may enter and leave the harbour regardless of the signals 'provided they proceed with caution and do not impede shipping in the main channel'. QHM harbour control is on VHF channels 11 and 13. Yachts should listen on channel 11.

Vessels under 20m must use the boat channel on the west side for both entry and departure. The boat channel

has northern and southern limits at the Ballast beacon (Fl.R. 2.5s) and No 4 Bar buoy (QR). With permission from QHM's port control (Ch11) the main fairway may be crossed when north of the port handed Ballast beacon. Thus north-going vessels should leave it to the west (i.e. to port), and south-going vessels to the east (i.e. to port).

THE FORTS

Spit Sand, Horse Sand and No Man's Land Forts might seem a bit too large and obvious to classify as hazards. Nevertheless in the past they were painted with black and white checks to make them more conspicuous to friendly shipping. They were built in the 1860s at vast expense to defend Portsmouth Dockyard against French invasion. It was originally intended that the inner fort should be on Sturbridge Shoal rather than Spit Sand but, after fairly extensive work on the foundations, it was discovered that the shoal was not firm enough. The same applied to a proposed fort on Ryde Sands. The designers wanted the sites so placed that ships in the channel would have to pass within 1000 yards of a fort, this being the range at which their guns could be sure to penetrate the heaviest armour used at that time. The protection and the armament of the forts themselves, particularly the two larger forts at Horse Sand and No Man's Land, is quite impressive, and it is clear that the defence of Portsmouth Harbour was taken seriously. For example the thickness of their stone lower walls is 18m. The original plan was to have forty-five 10-inch guns and forty-four 12.5-inch guns in the casements with another ten 12-inch guns on the roof. As if that was not enough, a controlled minefield was also laid between the two larger forts.

As one would expect, the names of the forts are derived from the banks on which they were built. Ancient charts and maps show three large offshore banks in the area of the eastern

entrance to the Solent called Horse Sand, No Man's Land and the Warner Shoal. It is not clear whether these banks ever dried out at low water, but it seems possible that they were a more distinct feature than they are today.

A fortuitous aid to self-sufficiency is that the forts are all provided with good quality fresh water from 120m deep artesian wells. The forts were put up for sale in 1963 but no buyers came forward until the 1980s. Spit Sand Fort was a restaurant and museum for a time but has been recently been sold, Horse Sand Fort was auctioned in October 1993, making £80,000, and No Man's Land Fort was made an object of a stunning-looking speculative development. A Chichester businessman sank a fortune into No Man's Land Fort when converting it into an unusual and exclusive fantasy home. There are enormous entertainment rooms, a revolving bed in the lighthouse suite, a tennis court, swimming pool, gymnasium, billiard room and three helipads, etc. All this, plus complete seclusion from the madding world and another 30,000 square feet of unconverted floor space, was on offer in 1990 for £5.75m. Only when the asking price came down to under £1m in 1993 was the fort, with all its lavish embellishments, eventually sold.

A good salty story comes from Tim Jeffreys, who anchored in a 34ft yacht close to Horse Sand Fort in gentle conditions a few years back. He was astonished to find that the anchor kept dragging however much chain was veered. Eventually the useless anchor was weighed with tremendous difficulty, only to find that it had acquired 45cm diameter wheels. The anchor had caught on the axle of what might have once been an ammunition trolley.

HORSE SAND BARRIER

The barrier between Horse Sand Fort and Southsea Beach consists of square concrete pedestals, of slightly variable

heights, which become partially exposed at low water spring tides (Plate 109). These were built in about 1905 to prevent an enemy from closing Portsmouth Harbour with a blockship, and would not be easy to remove. As intended, they are a menace, and trying to pass between them in a small craft towards low water without a chart or local knowledge is akin to Russian roulette. There is an account, for example, of the owner of a 10.7m yacht, a Nicholson 35, coming to grief on her maiden voyage, after striking one of the pedestals when slipping away in the evening with his secret lady friend. The rescue services went into action and by the time the couple had dried out ashore, the media had ensured that their secret was no more. The owner of the yacht is reputed to have said that he took the same route with his previous boat on the way in to Portsmouth Harbour, and was most surprised to encounter the barrier on his way out. His wife was not amused.

Beacons mark the concrete pedestals at regular intervals and there is a charted inshore boat passage, as well as the main passage half way between the fort and the Southsea shore.

109

Horse Sand Fort and the dangerous submerged barrier leading to Southsea Beach. The main passage can be seen towards the top of the photograph and a yacht approaching it from the south east.

NO MAN'S LAND FORT

Racing yachts are sometimes tempted to pass No Man's Land Fort very close on the north side and there have been reports of yachts grounding there at low water. This can be explained by the construction of both the No Man's Land and Horse Sand Fort walls, which are vertical above sea level but take the form of annular Portland stone or granite steps underwater. Moreover Army divers have found two girders extending up to 2m from the base of the south side of the fort, 1m above the seabed.

The above-surface barrier, shown on the chart as extending 610m to the south west of No Man's Land Fort, has long been removed. The piles on the Island side were driven into the seabed rather than set in concrete pedestals and were extracted after WW2, not without difficulty. Lingering doubts remained as to the safety of the channel south of No Mans Land Fort, sustained by the Hydrographer who, after the barrier was extracted, wisely left the indication of a 'submerged barrier' on the chart. The Queen's Harbourmaster Portsmouth of 2005 had all the obstructions removed, pronounced the channel clear and that there is now a minimum depth of two metres between the Radar (aka Debnigo) Post and No Man's Land Fort. The annotation 'foul bottom' informs users that this location is not suitable for anchoring. In order to leave the channel between No Man's Land Fort and Horse Sand Fort clear for shipping, small craft should use the channel inshore of No Man's Land Fort in preference to the main channel.

THE DEBNIGO

A long thin spit, called the Debnigo, extends like a snake from the Island shore at Puckpool Point towards No Man's Land Fort (Plate 110). The outer extremity of the Debnigo is marked by a red post that is still called Radar Post (light characteristic: long red flash every 12 secs) on account of the radar reflectors that used to be attached to it when it was located further west. The spit has moved a little way away to the east since the post was established but the post is still very useful as a reference. Inshore of the Radar Post there is a drain pipe from Spring Vale which, dependent on the considerable sand movement of the Duver, used to show from time to time above the sea bed between Nettlestone and Spring Vale. In 2000 the Spring Vale pipe was replaced and shortened from 686m to 90m, and is hardly a problem anymore.

110 (above)
The eastern tip of Ryde Sands with the Debnigo behind.

111 (Below)
Ryde Sands, looking southwest.

112

Looking east towards No Mans Land Fort. The outer spit of Ryde Sands can be seen in the foreground with Sandshead Post to the left of the tip.

RYDE SANDS

The great expanse of Ryde Sands (Plate 111) is horseshoe shaped with the opening facing east. Some charts do not show this clearly and it is possible to work up the inside and become embayed. A red post, called Sandshead Post (fl.R.10s) has been placed to the north of the eastern tip of the outer spit of sand (Plate 112). Having passed the post whilst working soundings along the north side of the spit, one should also watch out for the slightly more prominent sand banks (Plate 113) that have formed inshore. It is

113

A yacht aground on the outer spit of Ryde Sands. It was an opportunity to clean the yacht's bottom. Note All Saints Church on the skyline behind the yacht.

possible to cross Ryde Sands at high water, and there is no danger from the long sea outfall which goes from Appley right out to Sturbridge Shoal, as this is covered by at least 2m of sand. Older sewer pipes have long been removed to allow freer access to Ryde Harbour, which dries right out at low water. There are two short pipes to the east of Ryde Harbour marked ashore by posts with yellow crosses.

Having described in past editions the Southwest Mining Ground buoy as being useful for navigation, both mining ground buoys have now been permanently removed.

The popular drying Ryde Harbour (Plate 114) may be visited HW Ryde −2.5 to +2 hours and the most easterly of the three pontoons should be used by visitors. Ryde Harbour VHF is Ch 80.

114

Ryde Harbour at high water.

As one might expect, there is a prohibited anchorage area in the busy approach to Ryde Pier. A storm drain-pipe lies on the western side of the pier, marked by a red post. The outer end of the pipe is generally buried in the sand.

RYDE TO WOOTTON

There is not much tidal gradient to worry about over Ryde West Sands, and racing yachts often find they do best not far inside the edge of the shelf where there can be more wind. Binstead Rocks appear at low water off the thickly-wooded foreshore, called Players Beach, six cables to the west of Ryde Pier, making a natural harbour for small craft which can take the ground (Plate 115). The west end of the rocks is marked by a white post, which has been fitted with a red plastic float towards the top. The rocks used to split the moorings, but now all of the moorings are outside the rocks on the east side of the disused Binstead outfall. The seaward half of this old 0.6m sewer pipe projects a good metre above the seabed and is marked by a red buoy. The pipe is made of rolled steel and has become porous, but its supports are made of swamp forest wood and have lasted much better. To be sure of avoiding the pipe and its supports, one should keep to seaward

115

Binstead Rocks, Binstead outfall and Binstead Hard, looking south.

of the tall wooden post with a triple fork at the top, called Binstead Boom, which marks Binstead Hard. The probably man-made Binstead Hard juts well out into the Solent beside the pipe, opposite a large house called The Towers. Binstead is one of several possible landing points along this shore, a private high water landing being found at the Tacklers and Boating Club's jetty opposite the moorings. Given permission, the jetty is most convenient, and the hard might just about serve at low water. There are some boulders inshore near the hard, the most prominent of which is called Black Rock.

If one does land, one will notice near the jetty Seagull Cottage notable for a tunnel that, it is said, was one of several that once led to the old Quarr Abbey. From Saxon times to the early medieval period Binstead limestone was quarried in pits and shipped away for use in the construction of buildings: for example, Winchester Cathedral and the defensive walls of Southampton. On the beach evidence has been found of a wooden V-shaped fish trap, over 200m wide, which was constructed just before the Norman Conquest. Some wooden posts found on the Island shore have been so well preserved in the mud that the signatures of individual tools can be recognised on the sharpened tips.

WOOTTON

Though shallow, Wootton Creek has charm and offers a view of some of the quainter of Solent craft. There is a maintained depth of 3m for the ferry, but further up from the ferry terminal at low water the creek almost dries to a trickle in places.

When approaching Wootton Creek close to the shore from the east one should be aware of shingle banks that seem to be growing, roughly in line with the inner pair of beacons No 4 & 5 (Plate 116). It is of local interest that the banks now appear on a falling tide before the rocks on the west side. Movement of the shingle towards these banks from the shore has uncovered some Roman artefacts and buildings. To avoid the banks it is necessary to keep well outside the transit of Old Castle Point and a post on the west side of the channel. This post, which at the time of writing is adorned with a traffic cone, lies on the south side of the prominent and dangerous Wootton Rocks (Plate 117). The north side is now marked again with a red beacon.

Local boats use the inshore passage between Wootton Rocks and Wootton Point at high water. Further out from Wootton Rocks the Royal Victoria Yacht Club's starting platform will be seen by day, though not necessarily so by night, as it is not lit (Plate 118).

116

The banks to the east of Wootton Creek.

117 (above)

Looking southeast at Wootton Creek. Wootton Rocks are mid-way between the ferry and the RVYC starting platform, which can just be seen in the left foreground.

118 (left)

The RVYC starting platform from sea level.

Rather than skim along the shore, most visiting yachts will approach Wootton Creek along the starboard side of the dredged approach channel, keeping close to the beacons to be clear of the enormous ferries. Having passed the innermost beacon they quite reasonably steer directly for the starboard hand buoy ahead but alas, as the channel only takes a rather leisurely turn at this point, they frequently run aground on the starboard bank. One will avoid this mishap by heading initially for the port hand buoy or holding one's course until the triangular leading marks on the western shore are in line on 267°M. There is a speed limit of 5k within Wootton Creek.

WOODSIDE

Beyond Wootton there are small private jetties, useable at high water, at what used to be the Woodside holiday village, now closed. The flotsam-built easterly jetty, which flies a blue flag on an old dinghy mast, advertises a café to be found less than 100m inland, and presumably welcomes, or did once welcome, custom from passing craft (Plate 119). The orange cone buoy just to the east of the Woodside landings is one of the Royal Victoria Yacht Club's racing marks.

119

The beach near the disused Woodside holiday village.

KING'S QUAY CREEK

King's Quay Creek is a nature reserve (Plate 120) and, except in a dinghy, difficult to enter even at high tide. The area is privately owned and no landing is allowed. Nothing much has changed since 1928 when Adlard Coles called it 'hardly more than half a creek … but very attractive and unspoilt' (Plate 121).

There is a legend that says the name King's Quay Creek originated from a visit by King John who was seeking relaxation on the Isle of Wight after signing the Magna Carta. The story seems surprising as there was a civil war going on at this time and the Isle of Wight was not particularly loyal to the king. Nevertheless a colourful account of his visit has been well written up in the past.

The channel used to require entry from the west, but at the time of writing a more direct approach serves best. Keep the distant Rowridge TV tower central in the gap in the trees behind the creek, and then turn to port when close to the sandbank. The channel, known as 'The Gutter', is no more than 10m wide and scaffolding has been placed across the channel by the bridge to prevent access to the upper pool, though rowing dinghies can still pass through.

120

The approaches to Kings Quay Creek dry out completely at low water.

Kings Quay Creek.

PEEL BANK

Racing yachts frequently pass on the Island side of Peel Bank buoy to evade the main strength of the tide. At low water deep drafted-vessels should take care to avoid the shallow patches.

There is a red wreck buoy half a mile north east of King's Quay Creek. The 'wreck' was thought a piece of Mulberry harbour as this was once the WW2 anchorage, but new information suggests that it was a concrete coal lighter. It lies some 17m SSW of the buoy and used to show at extreme low water springs though now, probably, it

has started to crumble. One should note that the chart shows several patches on Peel Bank of less than 2m. These, which include the obstruction 0.35 mile to the east of Peel Bank Buoy shown as drying 1.4m, but more likely of charted depth 1.4m, are still thought to be fragments of Mulberry harbour. Apparently bits of steel rod stick out of them.

There is a designated, but rarely used, water ski area off King's Quay Creek with the Peel Wreck Buoy at its centre, and small white unlit buoys at the corners, marked 'ski'.

OSBORNE BAY

The pretty and wooded anchorage of

122

East Patch, between Kings Quay Creek and Osborne Bay.

Osborne Bay is sheltered from the prevailing wind and clear of the main tidal stream. In the late 16th Century it was called Mead Hole and was where the many flourishing pirates of the day brought in their plunder for resale. More recently it provided piers and a beach for Osborne House, which was Queen Victoria's home for many years.

Though shallow with many groynes and with reefs in the middle and at either end, it is a very popular but rather rolly anchorage in summer. The eastern of these reefs, East Patch, is shown on the chart off Barton Point (Plate 122).

Within the bay opposite the Tea House, as the large building on the beach with the central tower is known, the remnants of the Bathing Pier and West Patch extend over 400m out into the Solent. Though these lumps of masonry and rocks do not appear to lie much above the surrounding seabed level in some places, they do in others, as a Sigma 33 found to her cost on 9 November 2000. In any event the lumps do not provide a comfortable resting ground on which to dry out if caught by a falling tide.

At the western end of the bay there is a sandbank and a drying patch of rocks about 150m offshore (Plate 123). The rocks at the west end of Osborne Bay are of some consequence

123

Osborne Bay. Note the remnants of the Bathing Pier and the boat dried out near a patch of rocks at the west end not shown on the chart.

and are not shown on the chart. Some of them may be the remains of the Royal Pier aka HM Pier, which is shown on 19th Century charts.

Large signs declare that the beach is private and landing is prohibited, but there is some talk of visitors' moorings, building a new pier and opening up the beach to sea-borne visitors. That could make the magnificent Osborne House worth a visit. The house was built 1845-51 by Queen Victoria as her principal country retreat and remains very much as it was in her time.

NORRIS CASTLE TO THE SHRAPE MUD

Further west, yachts have been known to ground from time to time on the long finger of Norris Rocks (Plate 124), which are not well indicated on the chart. If working on soundings along the shore, Norris Buoy is too far offshore to be of help, but the west side of the gap in the woods marks the

124
Norris Rocks.

rock ledge splendidly. The rocks stand about a metre above the surrounding seabed level and, to be clear of the ledge, one should keep outside the line of Old Castle Point and (regrettably one can't do better than this) a tower-like clump of trees on the Beaulieu shore on a bearing of 296°M.

As one passes the crumbling sea wall on the way towards Old Castle Point (Plate 125), the one-time site of another Henry VIII castle, one should still keep an eye on the echo sounder as the sandy, boulder-strewn beach dries well out from the shore at low water spring tides. In 1990 a large new outfall was built off Old Castle Point running 700m in a northerly direction from the point. The diffusers are bee-hive-shaped concrete constructions which could foul an anchor, but a decision was made not to mark them, as it is not a suitable anchoring place, and any more buoys in this area would be confusing.

A contrary tide on the corner can drive the unwary inshore, ready to fall victim to a small rocky ledge off Castle Point (not shown on the chart) or,

125 (opposite page)
Looking southeast at the small patch of rocks off Old
Castle Point. Norris Rocks can be seen beyond.

more likely, on to The Shrape (Plate 126). This, at its seaward end, is a sand bank running about 200m west-northwest from the Norris Castle summerhouse, the lone square building on the shore. The bank rises quite sharply from the seabed, so as soon as the Ryde promontory disappears behind Old Castle Point a close eye should be kept on the echo sounder. At high water small craft can pass very close to the shore, but their helmsmen should be wary of the submerged wall leading out to sea from the westernmost corner of the summerhouse.

Past The Shrape, it is tempting to cut through the numerous small craft moorings on the way to the marinas or up the Medina River, but at low water many vessels will not have enough water and, to avoid running aground, will have to beat a retreat and enter the river between numbers 1 and 2 buoys. All this is expected to change when the Cowes Harbour breakwater is completed some time after 2009. There will be two entries into the harbour, one from the east and one from the west.

The speed limit, which is vigorously enforced in Cowes Week, is 6k, though this does not apply to the Red Jet ferries until they arrive within the entrance.

If berthing upstream, bear in mind that at one Cowes Week the floating bridge ferry became a severe embarrassment to a maxi yacht at low water spring tide. The twin ferry chains always lie at least 0.6m above the seabed in mid-channel and the helmsman of the maxi, having failed to drive over them at his first attempt, backed off and tried again at higher speed, only to become lodged between the two.

The Medina River, though not quite as pretty as other Solent rivers, is well-buoyed and has good transit lights at the south end. Many sailors will have reached the Folly Inn; and another option when gale-bound at Cowes is to make a high water expedition to Newport. Vessels with a draft of 2m should have no difficulty at springs. The river delivers mariners close to the centre of the town and gives an opportunity to visit the Classic Boat Centre. There is a big pontoon, good facilities – such as power, water and showers – and a convenient pub. If wishing to stay longer at Newport, single-keeled yachts can dry out alongside the quay wall, which will take half a dozen boats, and one can take the opportunity to scrub off. For this purpose the harbourmaster 01983525994 leaves out fender boards for visitors under the staircase of the harbour office.

126
Looking southeast at the sand spit at the north end of the Shrape Mud.

INDEX

ABOUT THE AUTHOR: *Peter Bruce*

Gold Roman Bowl, seven overall class wins at Cowes Week, besides a welter of other inshore and offshore races. He has had the distinction of winning his class in Cowes Week, Cork Week and the Scottish Series and the rare 'double' on winning the Britannia Trophy and New York Yacht Club Trophy at Cowes Week in 1988.

He enjoys cruising as much as racing, and has cruised his yachts to some of the remotest parts of the British Isles such as St Kilda, Loch Roag, and Inishbofin. Moreover he has cruised to Ireland, France, Spain, Belgium and the Netherlands.

After 24 years in the Royal Navy, Peter Bruce settled in the New Forest not far from Lymington, and continues to spend much of his life on the water. In the world of yachting he has become well known as a successful yacht racing owner, the revision author of *Heavy Weather Sailing,* author of local pilot books such as *Solent Tides, Solent Hazards, Wight Hazards* and *Inshore Along the Dorset Coast,* and a yacht helmsman and navigator of international calibre. He completed his first Fastnet Race in 1961 and since then has been in the British Admiral's Cup Team as helmsman, navigator and tactician on four occasions: on two of these in the winning team, and on a third in the top individual yacht. In his own boats *Genie, The Goodies* and sundry *Owls* he has won numerous national championships, the Round the Island Race

Peter Bruce's yacht *Owl.*

WIGHT HAZARDS

Peter Bruce's companion edition to Solent Hazards, covering the south sides of the Isle of Wight. The detailed information given, such as transits to clear rock ledges, and colour aerial photographs, allow small vessels to be navigated in confidence close to the shore. The A5-sized fourth edition, published in 2008, contains 92 pages and 120 photographs.

ISBN 978-1-871680-51-5

INSHORE ALONG THE DORSET COAST

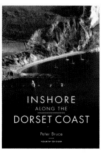

The highly praised mine of local knowledge by Peter Bruce, on the unusual, beautiful and interesting coast between Portland and Christchurch. The book has attracted a string of rave reviews and both mariners and cliff walkers have come to adore it. The A5-sized fourth edition was published in April 2008 with 136 pages and a 'feast' of 135 colour photos.

ISBN 978-1-871680-41-6

SOLENT TIDES

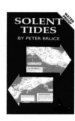

This popular tidal atlas, compiled by Peter Bruce, was a tremendous improvement upon Solent tidal stream information available up until this book was published, and has become another standard work of the Solent. It gives excellent detail, both in the main fairways and where eddies form along the shore. It is printed on durable plastic waterproof paper that is not only impermeable but is also almost impossible to tear. The third much revised A5-sized edition was published in 2008.

ISBN 978-1-871680-56-0

TIDAL STREAMS BETWEEN PORTLAND BILL AND ST. ALBAN'S HEAD

Modern technology has brought some new and very accurate tidal stream data to this popular coastline, thanks to HR Wallingford and Amoco, British Gas, BP and Elf. This tidal atlas by Peter Bruce and Gillie Watson is a big improvement on previous information available, particularly close inshore. Printed upon 18 pages of impermeable and tear resistant polyethylene A5-sized waterproof paper and published in January 1998.

ISBN 978-1-871680-16-4

All obtainable from:

BOLDRE MARINE
Kestrel Cottage • Shirley Holms
Lymington • Hampshire • SO41 8NH • UK
Telephone and Fax +44(0)1590683106

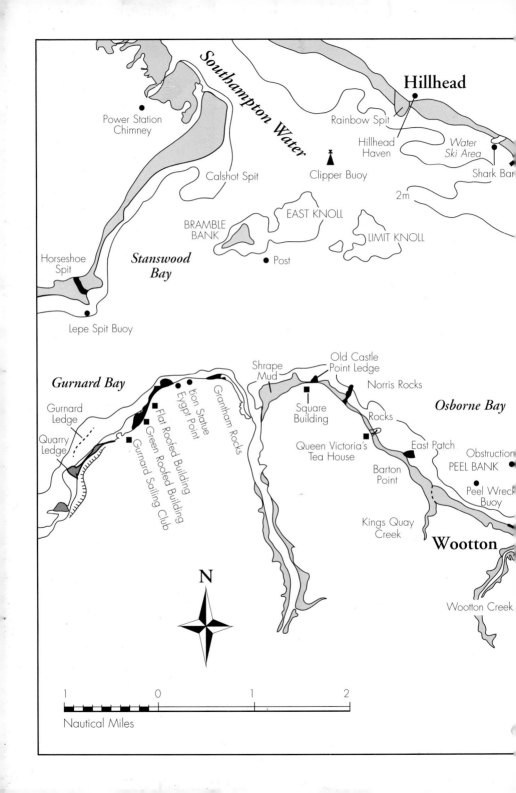